Deep Learning Methods for Automotive Radar Signal Processing

TECHNISCHE UNIVERSITÄT MÜNCHEN
Professur für Höchstfrequenztechnik

Deep Learning Methods for Automotive Radar Signal Processing

Rodrigo Pérez González

Vollständiger Abdruck der von der Fakultät für Elektrotechnik und Informationstechnik der Technischen Universität München zur Erlangung des akademischen Grades eines

Doktor-Ingenieurs

genehmigten Dissertation.

Vorsitzender: Prof. Dr.-Ing. Klaus Diepold
Prüfer der Dissertation:
1. Prof. Dr.-Ing. habil. Erwin Biebl
2. Prof. Dr. Reinhard Heckel

Die Dissertation wurde am 11.11.2020 bei der Technischen Universität München eingereicht und durch die Fakultät für Elektrotechnik und Informationstechnik am 01.03.2021 angenommen.

Bibliografische Information der Deutschen Nationalbibliothek
Die Deutsche Nationalbibliothek verzeichnet diese Publikation in der Deutschen Nationalbibliografie; detaillierte bibliografische Daten sind im Internet über http://dnb.d-nb.de abrufbar.

1. Aufl. - Göttingen: Cuvillier, 2021
Zugl.: (TU) München, Univ., Diss., 2021

Nonnenstieg 8, 37075 Göttingen
Telefon: 0551-54724-0
Telefax: 0551-54724-21
www.cuvillier.de

1. Auflage, 2021
Gedruckt auf umweltfreundlichem, säurefreiem Papier aus nachhaltiger Forstwirtschaft.

ISBN 978-3-7369-7462-3
eISBN 978-3-7369-6462-4

Abstract

The automotive industry is currently working towards bringing autonomous vehicles to the road. As the level of automated functions increase, so do the requirements for the vehicle's sensors and their corresponding algorithms. For fully automated driving to become a reality, future sensor systems must be able to not only reliably and accurately capture the vehicle's environment, but also to provide semantic information. Due to their cost and all weather robustness, radar sensors are an attractive candidate for this task.

In this work, deep learning methods, meant to enhance—or even replace—the classical radar signal processing chain, are developed and evaluated in the context of automotive applications. First a system that classifies pedestrians, cyclists and cars based on single-frame radar measurements is presented. It is a novel system, which demonstrates, that single-frame classification on the raw radar range-Doppler-angle spectrum with convolutional neural networks is feasible. The second classification approach presented in this work consists of performing a previous detection step to extract regions of interest of the range-Doppler-angle spectrum and then classifying them with a convolutional neural network, thus enabling multi-target scenarios.

A third system that replaces the detection, clustering, object creation and classification tasks is also presented. It employs the You Only Look Once (YOLO) object detection system—originally created for image object detection—on the radar spectrum. In one single step, the network provides a bounding box around the objects' range and velocity profiles and provides a class prediction. The fourth and last system, demonstrates the possibility of using artificial neural networks directly on the baseband time-domain signals for range detection. For this purpose, simulated targets are employed to train and evaluate the network. Furthermore, the approach is validated with real measurements.

Acknowledgements

This thesis is the result of my work of four years on a joint project of the Associate Professorship of Microwave Engineering of the Technical University of Munich and the BMW AG. I would like to take a moment to extend my gratitude to all the people, who contributed to its completion.

First, I would like to sincerely thank Prof. Dr. Biebl for giving me the opportunity to work on this very interesting and challenging project. I am very thankful for the liberty I enjoyed while working on this project, as well as for his readiness to help and excellent professional advice.

At BMW I would like to extend my gratitude to Dr. Ralph Rasshofer, who together with Professor Biebl first conceived the concept of this project. Likewise, I would like to thank Dr. Falk Schubert for mentoring me throughout the whole doctoral process. His frequent feedback, which often went beyond technical aspects, helped me greatly to steer my focus in the right direction. Furthermore, I would like to thank Dr. Qing Rao and Nick Engelhardt for their collaboration.

To Dr. Florian Pfeiffer from the company Perisens I extend my gratitude for the support in regards to high frequency measurements and radome design.

I am also very grateful to have shared this time with my colleagues at the Associate Professorship of Microwave Engineering Dr. Alois Ascher, Christian Buchberger, Bruna Cruz, Thomas Eder, Dr. Maximilian Engelhardt, Dr. Philipp Eschlwech, Michael Hani, Dr. Fabian Harrer, Onur Kepenek, Vera Kurz, Miroslav Lach, Felix Rutz and Dr. Nils Waldmann. The pleasing and friendly working atmosphere is something I valued dearly. Furthermore I'd like to especially thank Jana Mögel for her great support on all organisational matters and countless proofreadings.

Finally, I would like to thank all my friends, my parents Claudia and Eduardo and my brothers Emilio and Cristóbal for their unconditional support which has motivated me all along my academic path.

Contents

1 Introduction

Towards the end of the 19th century there were two events within the same decade that greatly influenced the way people travel and communicate nowadays. The first one takes place right at the beginning of 1886 in the city of Mannheim in Germany, where Karl Benz applied for a patent of his *Patent-Motorwagen* [Ben86]. The three-wheeled vehicle powered by an internal combustion engine is now widely regarded to be the invention of the modern car. Nowadays, motor vehicles play a fundamental role in modern society from transporting goods to personal travel and recreation. Alone in Germany, as of 2020 there are round 47.7 million registered passenger cars [Kra20]. Current vehicles are however vastly different to the ones produced at the end of the 1800s. Since then, substantial improvements have been made not only in powertrain technology and passenger comfort, but also in the safety systems for both passengers and bystanders. These systems can be generally divided in two categories: passive and active. The former category aims to minimize the severity of a collision and includes e.g. the seatbelt, the airbags and crumple zones. Active systems, on the other hand, are aimed at preventing the collision from happening in the first place. Examples from this category are the anti-lock braking system (ABS), autonomous emergency braking (AEB) and adaptive cruise control (ACC).

The second influential event happened a mere 50 kilometers away from the first one, in the city of Karlsruhe. There, the physicist Heinrich Hertz demonstrated the existence of electromagnetic waves. While their theory had already been laid out by James Clerk Maxwell in 1864, it was not until Hertz conducted a series of experiments between 1885 and 1889 that their existence was proven. This event gave birth to radio communications and its multiple applications, one of them being radar—an acronym for radio detection and ranging. The proto-radar sensor was introduced at the beginning of the 20th century by Christian Hülsmeyer. His *Telemobiloskop* [Chr04], as the sensing device was called, announced the presence of distant metallic objects within its line of sight and its intended use was to avoid the collision of ships. The following developments of radar systems were mainly driven by military necessity, e.g. for surveillance, navigation and weapons guidance [Ric14, pp. 2]. After World War II, civil applications of radar also started to emerge, e.g. weather radar, air traffic control, maritime navigation and by the end of the 20th century in series production cars.

At the beginning, automotive radar systems, such as *Distronic* on the Mercedes S-Class and *Active Cruise Control* on the BMW 7 Series, were used for ACC and were therefore mainly conceived with the comfort of the driver in mind [Gal16, pp. 296]. Later systems, such as AEB, are more concerned with increasing safety, i.e with the prevention of collisions. These kind of safety features are of utmost importance, since there is globally a high number of road traffic casualties. For example, in the EU, where

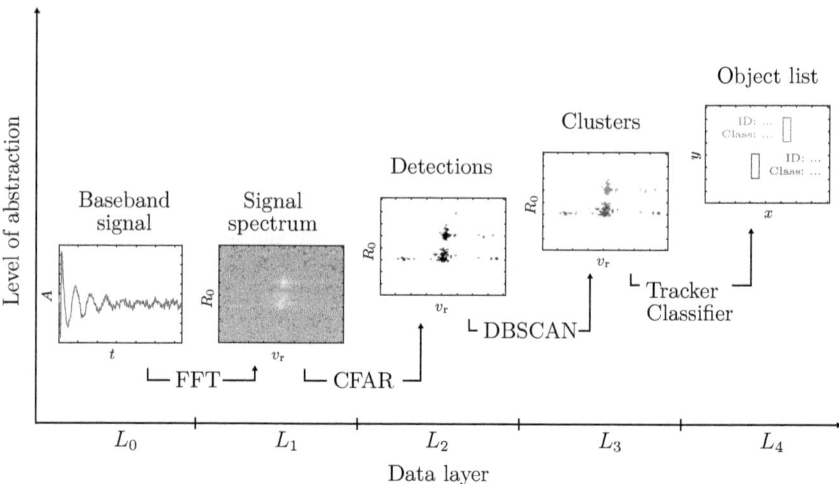

Figure 1.1: Abstraction levels at the different data layers of the classical radar signal processing chain.

the number of road fatalities decreased by around 40% in the span of 10 years, they still summed up to over 25,000 thousand in 2016 [Eur18a]. From this number, 8% is made up from bicycle fatalities [Eur18a] and 21% from pedestrian fatalities [Eur18b]. Pedestrians and cyclists are referred to as vulnerable road users (VRU), since the outcome of an accident is often more severe for them.

From the 21st century onwards, advanced driver-assistance systems (ADAS)—to which the previously mentioned active safety systems are part of—have become increasingly widespread and their functions more sophisticated. From automatic parking systems to blind spot detection and lane departure warning system (LDWS), the list is ever growing. To perform this tasks, radar sensors have become widespread in the automotive industry due to their low cost, high precision measurements of range, velocity and angle, and robustness in adverse weather and lighting conditions. The classical and simplified radar signal processing chain for automotive applications, divided in data layers at the crucial stages, is depicted in Fig.1.1. It all begins with the unprocessed time-domain baseband signal, which contains the information of the targets' range, velocity and angle in its frequency and phase components. By performing a fast Fourier transform (FFT), these frequencies are highlighted and, since the FFT is a linear and invertible function, no information is lost at this stage. A detection algorithm, e.g. constant false alarm rate (CFAR) detection, separates targets from noise and clutter. However, no detection algorithm is perfect, resulting in false positives as well as false negatives, and the higher level of abstraction at layer L_2 comes with information loss. Detections are then gathered in groups (clusters) at layer L_3 using algorithms such as

Table 1.1: The six levels of driving automation, as defined by the SAE International [J3018].

Level	Name	Description
0	No driving automation	All dynamic driving functions are fully performed by the human driver.
1	Driver assistance	Steering or accelerating performed by the driver assistance system under certain traffic situations.
2	Partial driving automation	Both steering and accelerating performed by the driver assistance system under certain traffic situations.
3	Conditional driving automation	The automated driving system performs all aspects of the dynamic driving task under certain traffic situations. The human driver is expected to respond appropriately to a request to intervene.
4	High driving automation	The automated driving system performs all aspects of the dynamic driving task under certain traffic situations, even when the human driver does not respond appropriately to a request to intervene.
5	Full driving automation	The automated driving system performs full-time all aspects of the dynamic driving task under all traffic situations and environmental conditions.

DBSCAN [EKS+96]. Some detections may also be discarded as noise during this stage. Lastly, high level algorithms produce predictions about the targets' attributes, e.g. their physical size, trajectories and classes. This is done based on features extracted at the highest abstraction levels.

For many of the ADAS, the classical radar signal processing suffices. They function mainly in simple and predictable situations, e.g. during highway drives or parking maneuvers. Nonetheless, the end goal in the automotive industry with regards to ADAS is to achieve fully autonomous vehicles. The road to reach this point has been divided into six levels of automation by the SAE International (Table 1.1). From levels 0 to 2, the human driver fully or partially performs the dynamic driving task. At level 2—where most modern vehicles are currently at—the automated driving system (ADS) can control both the steering and accelerating task under certain conditions. With "certain conditions" the previously mentioned simple situations are usually meant. Starting at level 3, the ADS is fully responsible for the dynamic driving task while engaged. Gradually a decreasing readiness of the driver to overtake control is needed until level 5 is reached, where a steering wheel is not even necessary.

With the increasing automation of driving functions comes an increasing demand for the sensors' capabilities. In order for autonomous driving to become a reality, the vehicle's sensors must be able to function in all kinds of scenarios, not only simple and predictable ones. Especially challenging is the situation presented by urban scenarios. These are more densely populated than motorway scenarios and also contain different types of road users, making them highly dynamic and more complex. For this reason, vehicles will have to accurately capture the environment and also understand it on a semantic level. With the ability to classify the different road users it then becomes possible to apply class specific prediction models, which outperform more general tracking approaches [DLS+19].

The last decade has seen an increase of deep learning techniques being applied to replace established methods across multiple disciplines. For example, in the computer vision domain, the classical approach of performing classification by extracting hand-selected features and then using a shallow classifier have been replaced by deep convolutional neural networks such as AlexNet [KSH12], VGGNet [SZ14] or GoogleNet [SLJ+15]. Also for object detection, approaches that combine the detection and classification in a single step—such as YOLO [RDGF15]—have become prevalent.

The problem of using manually designed features for object detections lies within finding robust ones that fit all kinds of objects with diverse appearance and in different illumination conditions and backgrounds [ZZXW19]. The same can be said about the parametrization of the different algorithms in the classical radar signal processing chain, e.g. of the detection and clustering algorithms, which must fit small and weak targets, such as pedestrians, as well as large and strong targets, such as trucks. Additionally, deep learning algorithms can make use of low-level information, usually discarded by the first steps in the signal processing chain, to perform high-level tasks, such as classification. For this reasons, deep learning has gained considerable interest in the automotive radar signal processing domain. The relevant developments in this area are introduced later in Chapters 4 and 5.

1.1 Goals and Contents of this Work

The goal of this work is to study the feasibility of using deep learning algorithms to enhance, or even replace, steps of the classical automotive radar signal processing chain depicted in Fig. 1.1. To do this, multiple detection and classification approaches, at different data layers of the radar signal processing chain, are developed and implemented.

First, the fundamentals of radar theory are introduced in Chapter 2. This includes the signal model, as well as the classical signal processing chain of continuous wave radar sensors. Additionally, the radar system and its parameters, which are used throughout this work, are presented at the end of the chapter.

Chapter 3 starts with the general theory and terminology of machine learning. After introducing the artificial neuron, deep learning with artificial neural networks and convolutional neural networks is described. Loss and activation functions, as well as common metrics used to evaluate the models in the following chapters are presented.

Two systems for the classification of VRUs are the subject of Chapter 4. A fundamental feature of both systems is the so called micro-Doppler effect, which is described at the beginning of the chapter. The first system is a novel—at the time of its publication—approach, which uses a convolutional neural network to perform classifications based on single-frame radar measurements. For this, only single-target and relatively simple scenarios are considered. The second system uses a detection procedure to extract regions of interest, which are then classified with a deep learning approach. In this case, the approach is multi-target capable and trained and evaluated with measurement data from test drives in inner city scenarios.

In Chapter 5, two detection systems, one based on time-domain signals (layer L_0) and one based on radar spectra (layer L_1), are presented. The system based on layer L_1 employs a state of the art single-shot object detector, known as YOLO, to simultaneously detect and classify VRUs on 2-dimensional radar spectra. It effectively replaces multiple steps of the radar signal processing chain with a single network: detection, clustering and classification. The second detection system is a novel approach, which runs the time-domain baseband signals through an artificial neural network, which performs detections on the range dimension, effectively replacing the fast Fourier transform (FFT) and the CFAR procedures in the classical signal processing chain.

Lastly, a summary of this work, concluding remarks and an outlook on possible future research are given in Chapter 6.

2 Radar Fundamentals

In this chapter the necessary theoretical background for radar sensors and radar signal processing is introduced. The scope of this work encompasses continuous wave (CW) radars only and for this reason the extent of the theoretical background is also limited to this class of sensors. Hardware aspects are mostly left out in order to focus on the signal models, which build the basis for the algorithms introduced in later chapters.

The derivation of the signal model begins with the simple mono-frequent CW radar, followed by the frequency modulated continuous wave (FMCW) radar and finally the chirp sequence FMCW radar. Following that, target detection procedures on the 2-dimensional radar spectrum are briefly described. These sections are mainly based on Kronauge [Kro14], unless otherwise specified. Furthermore, the signal model for performing angle measurements utilizing a phased array is derived following Richards [Ric14].

The last section in this chapter presents the chosen radar system, the waveform and system parameters selected to achieve the necessary performance in automotive urban scenarios, as well as the hardware modifications needed to integrate it in a test-vehicle.

2.1 Continuous Wave Radar

A radar sensor functions in the broad sense by radiating a high-frequency signal $s_{\mathrm{T}}(t)$ and receiving the backscattered signal $s_{\mathrm{R}}(t)$. The shape of $s_{\mathrm{T}}(t)$, also known as the *waveform*, is determined by the selected modulation scheme. This in turn will determine the characteristics of the radar system in regards to resolution, unambiguous measurement range and multi-target capabilities.

Figure 2.1 depicts the generic block diagram of a CW radar. A waveform generator is used to create a signal, which drives the voltage controlled oscillator (VCO). The VCO then produces the transmit signal, which can be analytically expressed as

$$s_{\mathrm{T}}(t) = a_{\mathrm{T}}(t) \cdot \cos(\phi_{\mathrm{T}}(t)), \tag{2.1}$$

where $a_{\mathrm{T}}(t)$ and $\phi_{\mathrm{T}}(t)$ denote the time dependent amplitude and phase of the signal. In the case of CW radars the amplitude is not modulated, i.e. the time dependent amplitude $a_{\mathrm{T}}(t)$ in Equation 2.1 becomes an arbitrary constant value, which is assumed to be equal to one ($a_{\mathrm{T}}(t) = 1$) to simplify further considerations. The instantaneous transmit frequency $f_{\mathrm{T}}(t)$ of $s_{\mathrm{T}}(t)$ is given by the time derivative of its phase:

$$f_{\mathrm{T}}(t) = \frac{1}{2\pi} \frac{\mathrm{d}\phi_{\mathrm{T}}(t)}{\mathrm{d}t}. \tag{2.2}$$

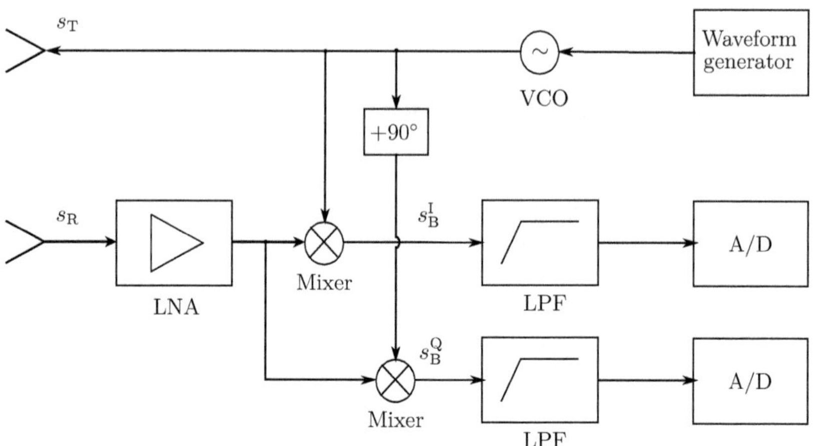

Figure 2.1: Block diagram of a CW radar.

The expression for the transmit signal in Equation 2.1 can then be re-written in terms of $f_{\mathrm{T}}(t)$ using Equation 2.2:

$$s_{\mathrm{T}}(t) = \cos\Big(2\pi \cdot \int_0^t f_{\mathrm{T}}(t')\mathrm{d}t'\Big). \tag{2.3}$$

If an object is present in the field of view (FOV) of the radar, the receive signal will constitute of the superposition of the backscattered transmit signal at different points on the object. In order to simplify the following derivations, it is assumed that only one point on the object scatters the signal back to the radar. The signal coming from the so called point-target at the radar receiver can thus be regarded as a time-delayed and scaled version of the transmit signal:

$$s_{\mathrm{R}}(t) = A_{\mathrm{R}} \cdot s_{\mathrm{T}}(t - \tau), \tag{2.4}$$

where τ is the round trip delay, i.e. the time that it takes for the signal to travel from the radar to the target and back again to the radar, and A_{R} is the amplitude of the signal. If the object is located at a range R_0 from the radar, the time delay is

$$\tau = \frac{2 \cdot R_0}{c}, \tag{2.5}$$

with the speed of light $c \approx 3 \cdot 10^8 \mathrm{m\,s^{-1}}$. The amplitude A_{R} is proportional to the received power P_{R}, which can be determined using the mono-static radar equation [Sko01, pp. 6]:

$$P_{\mathrm{R}} = \frac{P_{\mathrm{T}} \cdot G_{\mathrm{T}} \cdot G_{\mathrm{R}} \cdot \sigma_{\mathrm{r}} \cdot \lambda^2}{(4\pi)^3 \cdot {R_0}^4}, \tag{2.6}$$

where P_{T} is the transmit power, G_{T} the transmit antenna gain, G_{R} the receive antenna gain, σ_{r} the object's radar cross section (RCS) and λ the wavelength.

A CW radar simultaneously transmits and receives the backscattered signal. The receive signal is first amplified by a low noise amplifier (LNA) and then down-converted by mixing it with the transmit signal, which produces the intermediate frequency, also known as *baseband*, radar signal $s_{\mathrm{B}}(t)$. The block diagram in Fig. 2.1 contains an I/Q-mixer, which down-converts the in-phase and quadrature components of the receive signal separately. To simplify matters, the mixers can be regarded as ideal multipliers [Poz05]. In this case, the complex baseband signal can be expressed as

$$\begin{aligned} s_{\mathrm{B}}(t) &= s_{\mathrm{B}}^{\mathrm{I}}(t) - \mathrm{j}s_{\mathrm{B}}^{\mathrm{Q}}(t) \\ &= A_{\mathrm{R}}\Big[\cos(\phi_{\mathrm{T}}(t)) \cdot \cos(\phi_{\mathrm{T}}(t-\tau)) - \mathrm{j}\sin(\phi_{\mathrm{T}}(t)) \cdot \cos(\phi_{\mathrm{T}}(t-\tau))\Big], \end{aligned} \tag{2.7}$$

where $s_{\mathrm{B}}^{\mathrm{I}}$ and $s_{\mathrm{B}}^{\mathrm{Q}}$ are the in-phase and quadrature components of the complex baseband signal s_{B}. Using the formula for the product of trigonometric functions [BSMM08, pp. 82] the signal can also be written as

$$\begin{aligned} s_{\mathrm{B}}(t) = \frac{A_{\mathrm{R}}}{2}\Big[&\cos\Big(\phi_{\mathrm{T}}(t) - \phi_{\mathrm{T}}(t-\tau)\Big) + \cos\Big(\phi_{\mathrm{T}}(t) + \phi_{\mathrm{T}}(t+\tau)\Big) \\ &- \mathrm{j}\cdot\sin\Big(\phi_{\mathrm{T}}(t) - \phi_{\mathrm{T}}(t-\tau)\Big) + \mathrm{j}\cdot\sin\Big(\phi_{\mathrm{T}}(t) + \phi_{\mathrm{T}}(t+\tau)\Big)\Big] \end{aligned} \tag{2.8}$$

The subsequent low-pass filters (LPF) suppress the higher frequency components—those with $\phi_{\mathrm{T}}(t)+\phi_{\mathrm{T}}(t+\tau)$ in the argument—of the signal. Therefore, only the difference of the transmit and receive phases remains:

$$s_{\mathrm{B}}(t) = \frac{A_{\mathrm{R}}}{2}\Big[\cos\Big(\phi_{\mathrm{T}}(t) - \phi_{\mathrm{T}}(t-\tau)\Big) - \mathrm{j}\cdot\sin\Big(\phi_{\mathrm{T}}(t) - \phi_{\mathrm{T}}(t-\tau)\Big)\Big]. \tag{2.9}$$

Equation 2.9 can also be expressed using Euler's formula:

$$s_{\mathrm{B}}(t) = \frac{A_{\mathrm{R}}}{2}\exp\Big(\mathrm{j}(\phi_{\mathrm{T}}(t-\tau) - \phi_{\mathrm{T}}(t))\Big). \tag{2.10}$$

Finally, the signal gets digitalized by the analog-to-digital converters (ADC) so that the subsequent signal processing steps, e.g. detection, clustering or tracking, can be performed.

2.2 Mono-Frequent Continuous Wave Radar

The simplest form of a CW radar is the mono-frequent CW radar. For this kind of waveform, the transmit frequency remains constant at the center frequency f_{c} for the whole duration of the measurement. Figure 2.2 illustrates the transmit frequency of the mono-frequent CW radar for the duration of one measurement frame T_{m}.

Plugging $f_{\mathrm{T}}(t) = f_{\mathrm{c}}$ into Equation 2.2 yields the transmit signal for the mono-frequent continuous wave waveform (assuming a start phase of zero):

$$s_{\mathrm{T}}(t) = \cos\Big(2\pi\cdot f_{\mathrm{c}}\cdot t\Big). \tag{2.11}$$

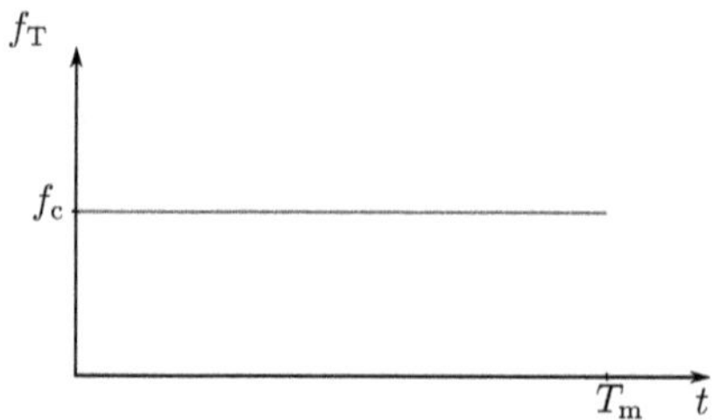

Figure 2.2: Transmit frequency of a mono-frequent CW radar.

Now, the scenario depicted in Fig. 2.3 is used to derive the range and velocity measurements characteristics of this waveform. Again, a point-shaped target assumption is made to simplify the derivations. The baseband radar signal originated by the running person is obtained by substituting $\phi_\mathrm{T}(t) = 2\pi \cdot f_\mathrm{c} \cdot t$ into Equation 2.10:

$$\begin{aligned} s_\mathrm{B}(t) &= \frac{A_\mathrm{R}}{2} \exp\Big(\mathrm{j}2\pi \cdot f_\mathrm{c} \cdot t - \mathrm{j}2\pi \cdot f_\mathrm{c} \cdot \tau(t) - \mathrm{j}2\pi \cdot f_\mathrm{c} \cdot t\Big) \\ &= \frac{A_\mathrm{R}}{2} \exp\Big(- \mathrm{j}2\pi \cdot f_\mathrm{c} \cdot \tau(t)\Big). \end{aligned} \tag{2.12}$$

Since the person is moving relative to the sensor with a radial velocity v_r, the distance becomes time-dependent and thus the round-trip time $\tau(t)$ does too:

$$\tau(t) = \frac{2}{c} \cdot \Big(R_0 + v_\mathrm{r} \cdot t\Big). \tag{2.13}$$

The radial velocity's sign is negative when the target is approaching the sensor (decreasing range and thus round-trip time) and positive when moving away from the sensor (increasing range and thus round-trip time). If the person's movement direction is not radial to the sensor, the radial component of their velocity vector $\boldsymbol{v}$ is given by

$$v_\mathrm{r} = |\boldsymbol{v}| \cdot \cos(\alpha), \tag{2.14}$$

where α is the angle between the heading direction of the person and the boresight direction of the radar.

Using Equations 2.12 and 2.13, the baseband signal can be expressed in terms of the radial velocity and the distance of the target:

$$\begin{aligned} s_\mathrm{B}(t) &= \frac{A_\mathrm{R}}{2} \exp\left(\mathrm{j}2\pi \cdot \left(- f_\mathrm{c} \cdot \frac{2v_\mathrm{r}}{c} \cdot t - f_\mathrm{c} \cdot \frac{2R_0}{c}\right)\right) \\ &= \frac{A_\mathrm{R}}{2} \exp\Big(\mathrm{j}2\pi \cdot \big(f_\mathrm{D} \cdot t + \phi_0\big)\Big), \end{aligned} \tag{2.15}$$

where

$$f_\mathrm{D} = -\frac{2v_\mathrm{r}}{c} \cdot f_\mathrm{c} \tag{2.16}$$

- Transmit signal (Tx)
- Receive signal (Rx)

Figure 2.3: Example scenario with a person running towards a car.

is the Doppler frequency and $\phi_0 = -f_c \cdot \frac{2R_0}{c}$ is a constant phase term. Since there is a direct relationship between the Doppler frequency and the radial velocity of the measured target, the mono-frequent waveform can be used to measure the relative radial velocity. Nonetheless, it is not possible to use this waveform to perform range measurements. While ϕ_0 is indeed related to R_0, it is only unambiguous within one wavelength, i.e. a fraction of a centimeter at a center frequency of 76.5 GHz.

2.3 Linear Frequency Modulated Continuous Wave Radar

In order to be able to perform range measurements with a continuous wave radar, the range information must be encoded within the phase $\phi_T(t)$ of the transmit signal. One way to do this is by modulating the transmit frequency $f_T(t)$, e.g. by linearly increasing it within the measurement time. The transmit frequency of the linear frequency modulated continuous wave (LFMCW) radar [KPDA60] is described by

$$f_T(t) = f_c + \frac{B_{sweep}}{T_{up}} \cdot t, \tag{2.17}$$

where B_{sweep} is the sweep bandwidth and T_{up} the frequency ramp—also called frequency *chirp*—duration. Figure 2.4 depicts the transmit frequency during one frequency chirp. Substituting $f_T(t)$ into Equation 2.3 yields the transmit signal of the LFMCW radar:

$$s_T(t) = \cos\left(2\pi \cdot \left(f_c + \frac{1}{2}\frac{B_{sweep}}{T_{up}} \cdot t\right) \cdot t\right). \tag{2.18}$$

Considering once again the scenario from Fig. 2.3, the baseband signal can be derived

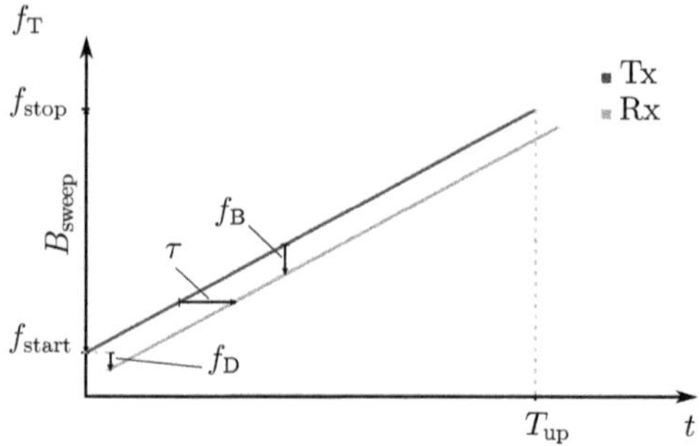

Figure 2.4: Transmit (Tx) and receive (Rx) frequency of an FMCW radar.

from Equation 2.10:

$$\begin{aligned} s_\mathrm{B}(t) = \exp\Bigg(\mathrm{j}2\pi\Bigg(\Bigg(-f_\mathrm{c}\frac{2}{c}v_\mathrm{r} - \frac{B_\mathrm{sweep}}{T_\mathrm{up}}\frac{2}{c}R_0 + \frac{B_\mathrm{sweep}}{T_\mathrm{up}}\frac{4}{c^2}R_0v_\mathrm{r}\Bigg)\cdot t \\ + \Bigg(-\frac{B_\mathrm{sweep}}{T_\mathrm{up}}\frac{2}{c}v_\mathrm{r} + \frac{B_\mathrm{sweep}}{T_\mathrm{up}}\frac{2}{c^2}{v_\mathrm{r}}^2\Bigg)\cdot t^2 \\ + \Bigg(-f_\mathrm{c}\frac{2}{c}R_0 + \frac{B_\mathrm{sweep}}{T_\mathrm{up}}\frac{2}{c^2}{R_0}^2\Bigg)\Bigg)\Bigg). \end{aligned} \tag{2.19}$$

The last equation can be simplified if all terms with the squared speed of light in the denominator, which are negligibly small, are ignored. Furthermore, the term $\frac{B_\mathrm{sweep}}{T_\mathrm{up}}\frac{2}{c}v_\mathrm{r}$, which describes the change over time of the beat frequency, can be neglected as well, under the condition that the sweep bandwidth is much smaller than the center frequency ($B_\mathrm{sweep} << f_\mathrm{c}$) [Kro14]. The baseband signal of the LFMCW is then reduced to

$$s_\mathrm{B}(t) \approx \exp\Bigg(\mathrm{j}2\pi\Bigg(-f_\mathrm{c}\frac{2}{c}v_\mathrm{r} - \frac{B_\mathrm{sweep}}{T_\mathrm{up}}\frac{2}{c}R_0\Bigg)\cdot t + \phi_0\Bigg). \tag{2.20}$$

Once again, as with the mono frequent CW radar, the constant phase term ϕ_0 cannot be used to retrieve the distance information due to its small unambiguous range.

Equation 2.22 contains two frequency components: the radial velocity dependent Doppler frequency f_D and a range dependent frequency term $f_\tau = -\frac{B_\mathrm{sweep}}{T_\mathrm{up}}\frac{2}{c}R_0$. The sum of these terms constitutes the observable frequency of the baseband signal, commonly referred to as the beat frequency f_B:

$$\begin{aligned} f_\mathrm{B} &= -f_\mathrm{c}\frac{2}{c}v_\mathrm{r} - \frac{B_\mathrm{sweep}}{T_\mathrm{up}}\frac{2}{c}R_0 \\ &= f_\mathrm{D} + f_\tau. \end{aligned} \tag{2.21}$$

The baseband signal can therefore also be expressed in terms of the beat frequency:

$$s_\mathrm{B}(t) = \exp\Big(\mathrm{j}2\pi\cdot f_\mathrm{B}\cdot t + \phi_0\Big). \tag{2.22}$$

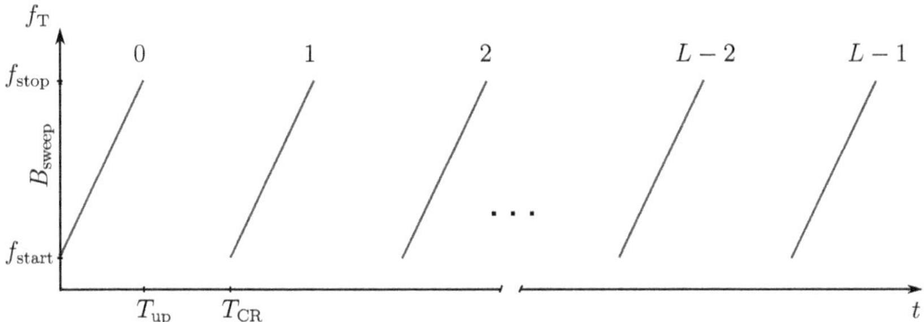

Figure 2.5: Transmit frequency of a chirp sequence FMCW radar.

If only a static scenario is considered, the beat frequency equals the range dependent component ($f_B = f_\tau$) and thus a range measurement can be performed by measuring the frequency of the baseband signal. However, if the target has a radial velocity component relative to the radar, the additional frequency shift due to the Doppler effect would introduce an error in the range measurement. It is not possible to separate the frequency components with this type of waveform and therefore to perform both range and velocity measurements. This problem is known as range-Doppler coupling [Ric14, pp. 178].

One way to overcome the range-Doppler coupling dilemma is to utilize an up-ramp, like the one depicted in Fig. 2.4, directly followed by a down-ramp. However, this would only help if there is only one single target present. For multi-target scenarios, a sequence of frequency chirps can be used to perform both range and velocity measurements.

2.4 Chirp Sequence Frequency Modulated Continuous Wave Radar

The transmit frequency of the chirp sequence FMCW radar is depicted in Fig. 2.5. Within a single measurement frame, L chirps are transmitted sequentially. This introduces a second dimension, from which the Doppler frequency f_D might be measured. The baseband signals obtained from each single chirp within a measurement frame must then only be processed coherently in order to be able to measure both f_B and f_D.

Once again, the scenario from Fig. 2.3 is considered. In this case, the round-trip delay is given by

$$\tau(t, l) = \frac{2}{c} \cdot \Big(R_0 + v_r \cdot (t + l \cdot T_{CR})\Big), \tag{2.23}$$

where T_{CR} stands for the chirp repetition interval, $l = 0, 1, \ldots L-1$ indexes the chirps within a measurement frame and $t \in (0, T_{CR})$. Using Equations 2.10, 2.17 and 2.23, the baseband signal for this scenario can be expressed as

$$\begin{aligned} s_{\mathrm{B}}(t,l) = \exp\bigg(\mathrm{j}2\pi\bigg(& -f_{\mathrm{c}}\frac{2}{c}v_{\mathrm{r}}\cdot(t+l\cdot T_{\mathrm{CR}}) - \frac{B_{\mathrm{sweep}}}{T_{\mathrm{up}}}\frac{2}{c}R_0\cdot t - f_{\mathrm{c}}\frac{2}{c}R_0 \\ & - \frac{B_{\mathrm{sweep}}}{T_{\mathrm{up}}}\frac{2}{c}v_{\mathrm{r}}\cdot(t+l\cdot T_{\mathrm{CR}})\cdot t \\ & + \frac{B_{\mathrm{sweep}}}{T_{\mathrm{up}}}\frac{2}{c^2}(R_0+v_{\mathrm{r}}\cdot(t+l\cdot T_{\mathrm{CR}}))^2\bigg)\bigg). \end{aligned} \tag{2.24}$$

Analogously to the single chirp LFMCW case, the terms on the second and third line of Equation 2.24 can be neglected, given that $B_{\mathrm{sweep}} << f_{\mathrm{c}}$ holds. Therefore, the baseband signal can be given in simplified form by

$$\begin{aligned} s_{\mathrm{B}}(t,l) &\approx \exp\bigg(\mathrm{j}2\pi\bigg(-f_{\mathrm{c}}\frac{2}{c}v_{\mathrm{r}}\cdot(t+l\cdot T_{\mathrm{CR}}) - \frac{B_{\mathrm{sweep}}}{T_{\mathrm{up}}}\frac{2}{c}R_0\cdot t - f_{\mathrm{c}}\frac{2}{c}R_0\bigg)\bigg) \\ &\approx \exp\bigg(\mathrm{j}2\pi\bigg(f_{\mathrm{D}}\cdot(t+l\cdot T_{\mathrm{CR}}) + f_{\tau}\cdot t + \phi_0\bigg)\bigg) \\ &\approx \exp\bigg(\mathrm{j}2\pi\bigg(f_{\mathrm{B}}\cdot t + f_{\mathrm{D}}\cdot l\cdot T_{\mathrm{CR}} + \phi_0\bigg)\bigg). \end{aligned} \tag{2.25}$$

After down-converting and low-pass filtering, the signals are sampled at the ADC with the sampling frequency f_{s}. The resulting discrete baseband signal can analytically be written as

$$s_{\mathrm{B}}(k,l) = \exp\bigg(\mathrm{j}2\pi\bigg(f_{\mathrm{B}}\cdot\frac{k}{f_{\mathrm{s}}} + f_{\mathrm{D}}\cdot l\cdot T_{\mathrm{CR}} + \phi_0\bigg)\bigg), \tag{2.26}$$

where $k = 0,1\ldots,K-1$ stands for the sample index within one chirp. The total number of samples in one chirp is dependent on the sampling frequency and the chirp duration ($K = T_{\mathrm{up}}\cdot f_{\mathrm{s}}$).

From Equation 2.26 can be seen, that by holding l constant, i.e. by considering a single chirp, and evaluating the function across the k axis, the beat frequency is observed. On the other hand, if $s_{\mathrm{B}}(k,l)$ is evaluated for a constant value of k, the Doppler frequency is observed. This can be achieved by computing the discrete Fourier transform (DFT) across each axis independently:

$$S_{\mathrm{B}}(n,m) = \sum_{l=0}^{L-1}\sum_{k=0}^{K-1} s_{\mathrm{B}}(k,l)\cdot\exp\bigg(-\mathrm{j}2\pi\frac{k\cdot n}{K}\bigg)\cdot\exp\bigg(-\mathrm{j}2\pi\frac{l\cdot m}{L}\bigg), \tag{2.27}$$

where $n = -K/2,\ldots,K/2-1$ indexes the discrete beat frequency bins and $m = -L/2,\ldots,L/2-1$ the discrete Doppler frequency bins. The frequency-domain baseband signal S_{B} in Equation 2.27 is also known as the range-Doppler spectrum. In practice, an FFT algorithm is used to compute the DFT more efficiently, e.g. the Cooley-Tukey algorithm [CT65], which reduces the complexity from $\mathcal{O}(N^2)$ to $\mathcal{O}(N\log N)$ if the length N is a power of 2. The general chirp sequence FMCW radar signal processing chain, from the transmitted wave up until the second FFT is depicted in Fig. 2.6.

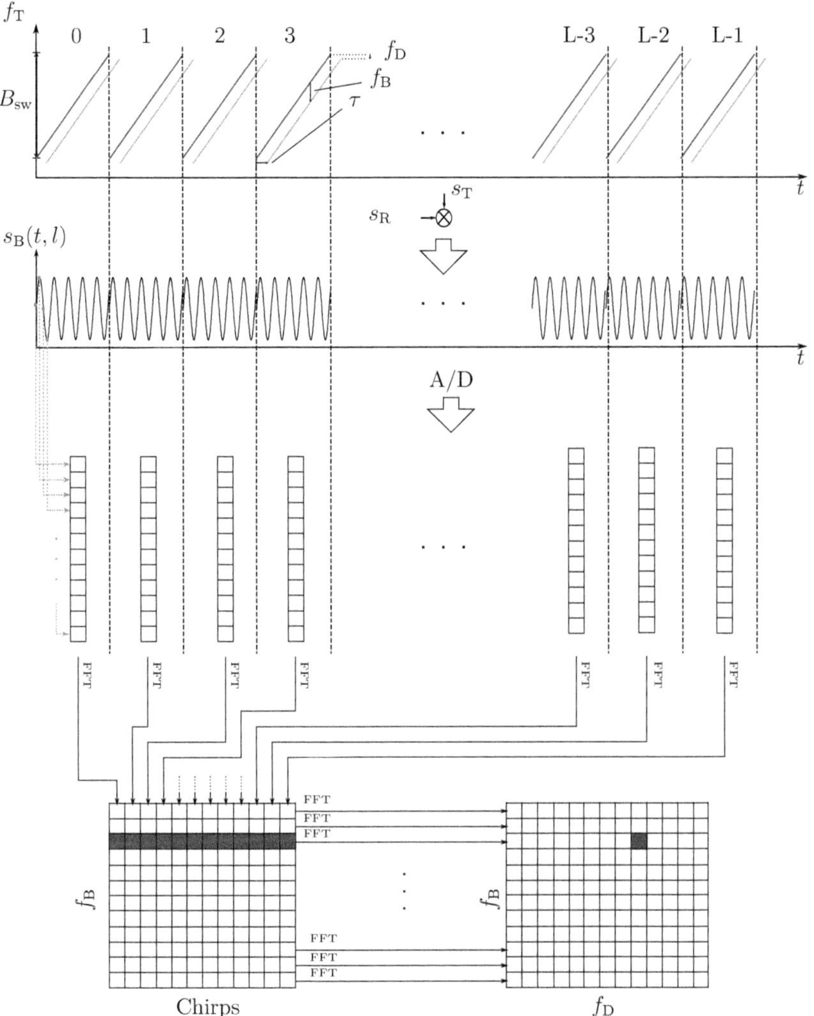

Figure 2.6: Chirp sequence FMCW radar signal processing chain.

In order to resolve targets in range and velocity dimensions, the corresponding beat and Doppler frequencies must appear as two distinct peaks in the range-Doppler spectrum. In the case of the beat frequency, its resolution Δf_{B} is inverse proportional to the chirp duration:

$$\Delta f_{\mathrm{B}} = \frac{1}{T_{\mathrm{up}}}. \tag{2.28}$$

Therefore, for two targets with the same radial velocity but different ranges the minimum distance from one another in range dimension at which they can still be resolved is given by

$$\begin{aligned} \Delta R_0 &= \frac{T_{\mathrm{up}}}{B_{\mathrm{sweep}}} \frac{c}{2} \Delta f_{\mathrm{B}} \\ &= \frac{c}{2 \cdot B_{\mathrm{sweep}}}. \end{aligned} \tag{2.29}$$

In the same manner, the radial velocity resolution can be derived. The Doppler frequency resolution Δf_{D} is dependent in this case on the total frame duration $L \cdot T_{\mathrm{CR}}$:

$$\Delta f_{\mathrm{D}} = \frac{1}{L \cdot T_{\mathrm{CR}}}. \tag{2.30}$$

The radial velocity resolution is therefore

$$\begin{aligned} \Delta v_{\mathrm{r}} &= \frac{c}{2 \cdot f_{\mathrm{c}}} \cdot \Delta f_{\mathrm{D}} \\ &= \frac{c}{2 \cdot f_{\mathrm{c}}} \cdot \frac{1}{L \cdot T_{\mathrm{CR}}}. \end{aligned} \tag{2.31}$$

Also of interest are the maximum unambiguously measurable range $R_{0,\mathrm{max}}$ and radial velocity $v_{\mathrm{r,max}}$. According to the sampling theorem [Sha49], a signal can be reconstructed from discrete samples as long as its frequency band is limited to half the sampling frequency. This condition is also known as the Nyquist criterion. Any frequencies higher than that would result in frequency aliasing [Lyo10, pp. 38-42]. As a consequence of this, the maximum beat frequency, which can be unambiguously measured, is limited by the sampling frequency f_{s}:

$$f_{\mathrm{B,max}} = \frac{f_s}{2}. \tag{2.32}$$

For a static target ($f_{\mathrm{D}} = 0$), the maximum measurable range is given by:

$$\begin{aligned} R_{0,\mathrm{max}} &= \frac{T_{\mathrm{up}}}{B_{\mathrm{sweep}}} \frac{c}{2} \cdot f_{\mathrm{B,max}} \\ &= \frac{T_{\mathrm{up}}}{B_{\mathrm{sweep}}} \frac{c}{2} \cdot \frac{f_s}{2}. \end{aligned} \tag{2.33}$$

The same principle applies to the measurement of the Doppler frequency. The baseband signal $s_{\mathrm{B}}(k,l)$ is sampled across the l-axis with the chirp repetition frequency

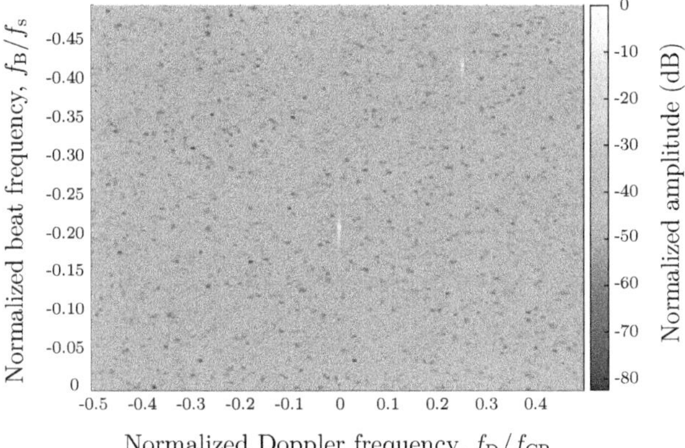

Figure 2.7: An example with a static and a moving target showing aliasing in the Doppler frequency. The moving target has a true Doppler shift of $-0.75 \cdot f_{CR}$, i.e. it is moving away from the radar sensor. However, it appears as a target with a Doppler shift of $0.25 \cdot f_{CR}$, i.e. as if it were moving towards the sensor.

$f_{CR} = 1/T_{CR}$. From the sampling theorem follows for the absolute value of the maximum unambiguous Doppler frequency:

$$|f_{D,max}| = \frac{f_{CR}}{2}. \tag{2.34}$$

Consequently, the maximum unambiguously measurable absolute radial velocity becomes:

$$\begin{aligned} |v_{r,max}| &= \frac{c}{2 \cdot f_c} \cdot |f_{D,max}| \\ &= \frac{c}{4 \cdot f_c} \cdot \frac{1}{T_{CR}}. \end{aligned} \tag{2.35}$$

The low pass filters in Fig. 2.1 function as anti-aliasing filters, since they suppress frequency components above $f_s/2$. For this reason, aliasing in the beat frequency dimension is usually not a problem, given that the low pass filters provide sufficient stopband suppression. However, for the Doppler frequency dimension it is not possible to low pass filter the signal before sampling, since the signal is already time-discrete from the beginning. Therefore, aliases of radial velocities outside of the unambiguous range will show up in the range-Doppler spectrum. Figure 2.7 depicts an example of this phenomenon. One possible way to circumvent this problem is to use a frequency shift keying chirp sequence waveform [KR14].

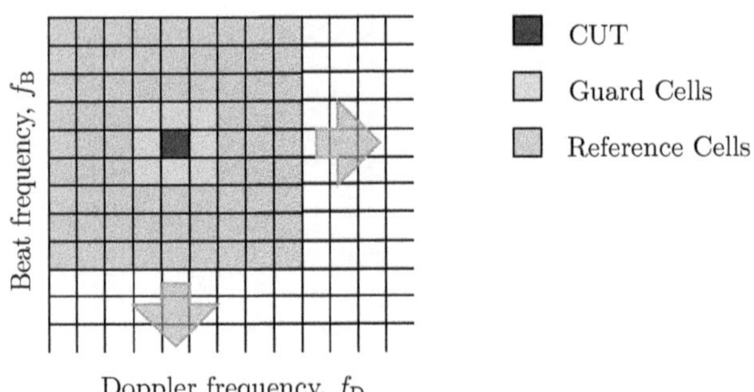

Figure 2.8: Sliding reference window used to estimate the noise level in a CFAR detection procedure. Based on [Kro14].

2.5 Target Detection

The task of target detection consists of setting a threshold T, which separates peaks originated by a target from noise and clutter on the radar spectrum. Since the noise level is usually unknown and constantly changing due to different environment conditions, a method to continuously estimate it is needed. Based on the noise level estimate, the threshold can then be set to meet certain conditions. A common method for adaptive threshold selection in radar signal processing is constant false alarm rate (CFAR) detection. As the name suggests, a threshold set by a CFAR procedure will result in a constant rate of false alarms, which can be parameterized as desired.

The starting point of this kind of procedure is the 2-dimensional—or one dimensional in the case of sole range detections—power spectrum

$$P_{\mathrm{B}}(n,m) = |S_{\mathrm{B}}(n,m)|^2. \tag{2.36}$$

When testing if a cell on the spectrum contains a target, a 2-dimensional window around the cell under test (CUT) is used as a reference to estimate the noise level Z. Figure 2.8 depicts the sliding window on the range-Doppler power spectrum. Subsequently, the threshold for the CUT is calculated by multiplying the noise level estimate with a scaling factor:

$$T = \beta \cdot Z. \tag{2.37}$$

The exact method to estimate Z from the reference cells as well as how to compute the scaling factor β to achieve a certain false alarm probability P_{fa} depend on the specific constant false alarm rate (CFAR) variation. Here, two of the more popular variations, cell averaging (CA) CFAR and order statistics (OS) CFAR, are briefly described.

2.5.1 Cell Averaging CFAR

In the case of CA-CFAR, the noise level estimate is obtained by computing the average power level of all reference cells:

$$Z_{\mathrm{CA}} = \frac{1}{N \cdot M} \sum_{m=1}^{M} \sum_{n=1}^{N} P_{\mathrm{B}}(n, m), \tag{2.38}$$

where N and M are the size of the reference window in the beat frequency and Doppler frequency dimensions. The scaling factor β_{CA} is determined by selecting the desired P_{fa} and solving the following equation [Ric14, pp. 341]:

$$P_{\mathrm{fa}} = \frac{1}{(1 + \frac{\beta_{\mathrm{CA}}}{N})^N}. \tag{2.39}$$

The guard cells in Fig. 2.8 are needed for the CA-CFAR procedure, in order to avoid raising the threshold by the falling slope of a peak. The main problem of this CFAR variant arises when multiple targets fall inside the reference window. For example, if a weak target is at the CUT, while a much stronger target is in a reference cell, the threshold will be raised, effectively masking the target in the CUT.

2.5.2 Order Statics CFAR

For OS-CFAR detection, the noise estimate is done by sorting all cells inside the reference window in ascending order and selecting the κ-th value, also known as the κ-th order statistic, as an estimate for the noise level:

$$Z_{\mathrm{OS}} = P_{\mathrm{B}(\kappa)}. \tag{2.40}$$

The scaling factor for the OS-CFAR detector is then approximated numerically to satisfy the following equation, since a closed solution does not exist [Roh83]:

$$P_{\mathrm{fa}} = \frac{N!}{(N-\kappa)!} \frac{(\beta_{\mathrm{OS}} + N - \kappa)!}{(\beta_{\mathrm{OS}} + N)!}. \tag{2.41}$$

If the κ-th value is chosen appropriately, the masking problem by a strong target within the reference window can be mitigated. For this, the number of interfering targets in a reference window should not exceed the difference between the total number of reference cells and the chosen rank [Ric14, pp. 356]. The use of guard cells is also not necessary, since they are rejected by an appropriate choice of κ [Kro14, pp. 108]. A big drawback from OS-CFAR is the computing effort necessary to sort the values of the reference cells. A combination of OS and CA CFAR techniques, which reduce the computing time considerably, can be found in [KR13].

2.6 Phased Arrays

So far, all derivations have been made assuming that the radar system has only one receive channel. However, if one desires to measure the azimuth or elevation angle of targets in respect to the radar sensor, multiple spatially separated receivers are needed. Below, the angle measurement is derived for the azimuth direction. The elevation angle measurement can be derived analogously. Further, it is assumed that the waves arriving at the array are plane waves. This assumption is valid, if the source of the wave is located in the far field of the antenna array [Cad90], which is satisfied for ranges greater than the Fraunhofer distance [Sil84, pp. 199]

$$R_{\mathrm{Fra}} = \frac{2D^2}{\lambda}, \tag{2.42}$$

where D is the dimension of the radiator, i.e. of the antenna or antenna array.

The simplest arrangement of multiple receive antennas is the uniform linear array (ULA). In this kind of array, the single antenna elements are spanned across one axis and separated from each other by a distance d. Figure 2.9 depicts a plane wave impinging at an angle θ on a ULA with U antenna elements. The additional distance the wavefront has to travel to arrive at the u-th element ($u = 0, 1, \ldots, U-1$) results in a phase shift given by

$$a(u,\theta) = \exp\left(-\mathrm{j}2\pi \cdot \frac{d \cdot \sin\theta}{\lambda} u \right) = \exp\left(\mathrm{j}2\pi \cdot f_\theta \cdot u \right), \tag{2.43}$$

where $f_\theta = -d \cdot \sin\theta / \lambda$ stands for the normalized spatial frequency in cycles per sample as projected into the plane of the array face [Ric14, pp. 516]. Combining Equations 2.26 and 2.43 yields the baseband signal at the u-th receiver of a chirp sequence FMCW radar:

$$s_{\mathrm{B}}(k,l,u) = \exp\left(\mathrm{j}2\pi \left(f_{\mathrm{B}} \cdot \frac{k}{f_{\mathrm{s}}} + f_{\mathrm{D}} \cdot l \cdot T_{\mathrm{CR}} + f_\theta \cdot u + \phi_0 \right) \right). \tag{2.44}$$

In the same way the beat and Doppler frequencies can be measured by observing $s_{\mathrm{B}}(k,l,u)$ along the k and l axis, the normalized spatial frequency and thus θ can be measured by observing $s_{\mathrm{B}}(k,l,u)$ along the u axis. The three-dimensional range-Doppler-angle spectrum $S_{\mathrm{B}}(n,m,w)$ is thus obtained by performing 3 independent FFTs:

$$\begin{aligned} S_{\mathrm{B}}(n,m,w) = \sum_{u=0}^{U-1} \sum_{l=0}^{L-1} \sum_{k=0}^{K-1} s_{\mathrm{B}}(k,l,u) \cdot \exp\left(-\mathrm{j}2\pi \frac{k \cdot n}{K} \right) \cdot \exp\left(-\mathrm{j}2\pi \frac{l \cdot m}{L} \right) \\ \cdot \exp\left(-\mathrm{j}2\pi \frac{u \cdot w}{U} \right), \end{aligned} \tag{2.45}$$

where $w = -U/2, \ldots, U/2-1$ are the normalized spatial frequency bins. Since both time-domain and frequency-domain baseband signals can be arranged as a three dimensional data structure (see Fig. 2.10), they are also known as radar *datacubes*. Often, the datacube is expressed as a power spectrum:

$$P_{\mathrm{B}}(n,m,w) = |S_{\mathrm{B}}(n,m,w)|^2. \tag{2.46}$$

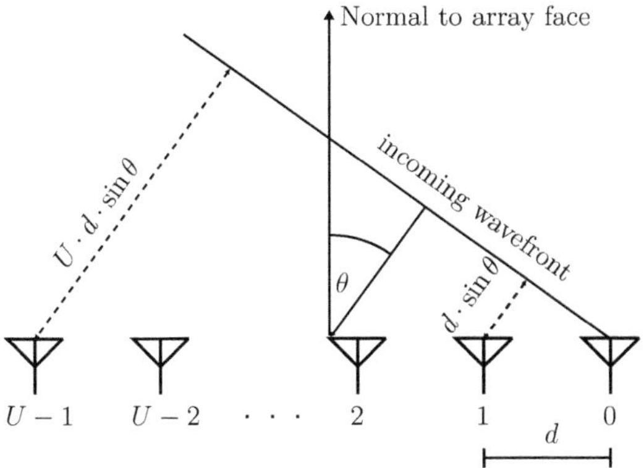

Figure 2.9: Wavefront impinging at angle θ on a V-element uniform linear array. Adapted from [Ric14].

By having multiple antennas, the signal is effectively being sampled in space. For this reason, the physical spacing between the array elements will affect the ability to unambiguously determine the angle of arrival (AOA) of a wave. The spatial frequency is defined as [Ric14, pp. 125]

$$F_x = \frac{\sin\theta}{\lambda}. \tag{2.47}$$

Since the AOA θ ranges between $-90°$ and $90°$ ($-\pi/2\,\mathrm{rad}$ and $\pi/2\,\mathrm{rad}$), it follows that the range of the spatial frequency is from $-1/\lambda$ to $1/\lambda$. Consequently, the total spatial "bandwidth" of the signal is

$$\beta_x = \frac{2}{\lambda}. \tag{2.48}$$

In order to satisfy the Nyquist criterion and thus avoid aliasing of the spatial frequency, the following condition for the sampling intervals applies:

$$d \leq \frac{1}{\beta_x} = \frac{\lambda}{2}. \tag{2.49}$$

This means that the antenna elements of the array should not be positioned further than half a wavelength from each other.

The angular resolution of the ULA is equal to its half-power beamdwidth $\theta_{3\mathrm{dB}}$. According to Richards [Ric14, pp. 14], it can be approximated by

$$\theta_{3\mathrm{dB}} \approx 0.89\frac{\lambda}{U \cdot d}, \tag{2.50}$$

given that the array contains a sufficient number of elements (9 or more). For a spacing of $d = \lambda/2$ the half-power beamwidth becomes

$$\theta_{3\mathrm{dB}} \approx \frac{1.78}{U}. \tag{2.51}$$

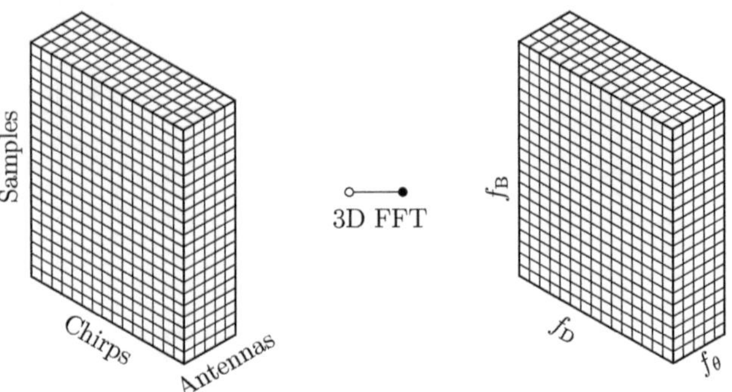

Figure 2.10: Time-domain datacube and frequency-domain datacube.

Superresolution methods such as MUSIC or ESPRIT are able to achieve better resolution than the one given by the last equation. They are however outside of the scope of this work. For an overview of multiple AOA algorithms, the reader is referred to the work of Krim and Viberg [KV96].

2.7 Radar System Considerations

There are multiple factors that need be considered for the choice of the radar system. To begin with, the system parameters should be as close as possible to the requirements in the automotive industry. Additionally, the sensor should provide an interface to access the raw radar data, i.e. the sampled time-domain signals, as modeled in Equation 2.44. Likewise, the achieved range and velocity resolutions must be able to separate the micro-Doppler components, later discussed in Section 4.1. Lastly, the sensor must be able to operate while integrated in a test vehicle, which means that an appropriate case to protect it from water and debris must be found.

2.7.1 Experimental Radar Board

The first parameter to choose is the operational frequency of the radar system. For automotive applications there are currently four frequency bands available in the European Union: one centered at 24.15 GHz, one at 24.25 GHz, one at 76.5 GHz, and one at 79 GHz.

The first of the group of the lower frequency bands is the industry, scientific and medical (ISM) narrow-band spanning from 24.05 GHz to 24.25 GHz. The 200 MHz bandwidth results in a maximum achievable range resolution of $\Delta R_0 \approx 75$ cm, which is not sufficient for urban automotive scenarios and is therefore more commonly found in industry applications [HTS+12]. The second option is the ultra wide band (UWB) 24 GHz frequency band, which ranges from 21.65 GHz to 26.65 GHz [ETS17b]. While it provides a total bandwidth of 5 GHz, it will nonetheless be phased out at the end of 2021. This leaves both frequency ranges out of consideration.

Both remaining frequency bands are centered at substantially higher frequencies, which comes with some essential advantages. First, since the velocity resolution is inverse proportional to the center frequency (see Equation 2.31), they provide a better basis for observing the aforementioned micro-Doppler features. The same applies for angular resolution: arrays of the same physical dimensions achieve better angular resolution at higher frequencies (see Equations 2.50 and 2.51). This also means that the form factor of the sensor can be reduced without sacrificing performance, which is vital for the integration into a vehicle.

At 76.5 GHz the allocated frequency bandwidth is 1 GHz, which translates to a range resolution of $\Delta R_0 \approx 15\,\mathrm{cm}$. With this resolution it is possible to more finely capture the environment the car is driving in, e.g. detecting multiple reflections on a cyclist driving in front of the car. The regulations also permit a high equivalent isotropic radiated power (EIRP) [ETS16] and for this reason it has been established as the frequency band for long range radar.

The 77–81 GHz allocated frequency range [ETS17a] serves as a replacement of the 24 GHz UWB. With its large bandwidth and high center frequency it achieves excellent range and velocity resolutions. The maximum allowed EIRP is not as high as in the 76.5 GHz band, which makes it more suitable for mid-range radar.

Since the intended measurement scenarios are urban traffic scenarios, the most apt frequency band would be the 79 GHz UWB. However, the technology is not as mature as in the 76.5 GHz case and no commercial radar evaluation boards were available at the beginning of this project. Therefore, the 76.5 GHz remains as the only viable option. As already mentioned, the sensor should have access to the unprocessed time-domain signals, which rules most *Tier 1* suppliers out. This level of access is mostly only provided by so called radar evaluation boards, which are intended for research and development and not for actual use in series products. The *radarbook* from INRAS is one of those radar evaluation platforms. It can be paired with a 77 GHz frontend [Inr15b]—also provided by INRAS—with multiple transmit and receive channels. Additionally, it allows for freely configuration of the radar waveform. For these reasons the *radarbook* is chosen as the radar sensor used throughout this work.

2.7.2 Waveform Design

The *radarbook* allows for either single or multiple chirp waveforms. Since the velocity axis is needed, only a chirp sequence comes into consideration. There are four values that need to be considered when parameterizing the radar waveform: the range resolution ΔR_0, the velocity resolution Δv_r, the maximum unambiguously measurable range $R_{0,\mathrm{max}}$, and the maximum unambiguous measurable velocity $v_{\mathrm{r,max}}$. The relevant waveform parameters that can be configured on the radar evaluation board to adjust these last values are the sweep Bandwidth B_sweep, the ramp up-time T_up, the chirp repetition interval T_CR, the number of chirps within a measurement frame L, and the sampling frequency f_s.

a) **Range resolution.** On the grounds that ΔR_0 can only be affected by changing the sweep bandwidth, it is the first parameter to be set. The full allocated bandwidth of 1 GHz is used, in order to be able to resolve multiple reflection points on subjects such as pedestrians and cyclists.

b) **Velocity resolution.** Previous investigations on the human gait use velocity resolutions ranging from $\Delta v_r = 0.025\,\mathrm{m\,s^{-1}}$ to $\Delta v_r = 0.18\,\mathrm{m\,s^{-1}}$ [SMKM15b], [FRR06], [vG03]. Schubert et al. assume a lower bound for the velocity resolution of $0.2\,\mathrm{m\,s^{-1}}$ to allow for separability of at least two prominent points of the gait cycle [SKFM14]. According to Equation 2.31, Δv_r is inverse proportional to the chirp sequence duration, i.e. to T_{CR} and L. The radar board allows for a maximum of $L = 256$ adjacent frequency ramps within one measurement frame and this value is therefore selected. By choosing a chirp repetition interval of $T_{CR} = 64\,\mu s$, a velocity resolution of $\Delta v_r = 0.12\,\mathrm{m\,s^{-1}}$ can be achieved. This value lies well within the previously mentioned interval found in the literature.

c) **Max. unambiguously measurable range.** $R_{0,max}$ depends on the maximum measurable beat frequency f_B and thus on the sampling frequency f_s. The *radarbook* has two analog front ends (AFE), whose ADCs can sample at a maximum rate of 80 MHz, for sampling the baseband signal. Each AFE samples 4 channels sequentially, thus the maximum sampling frequency of one channel is 20 MHz. However, when working at the maximum possible frequency, performance issues were encountered. A stable performance was achieved at a sample frequency of $f_s = 10\,\mathrm{MHz}$. Increasing T_{up} would result in a higher $R_{0,max}$, however it would also effectively increase T_{CR} and consequently decrease $v_{r,max}$. A good trade off is found at $T_{up} = 32\,\mu s$ resulting in $R_{0,max} = 23.85\,\mathrm{m}$, which is acceptable for the urban scenarios investigated in this work.

d) **Max. unambiguously measurable velocity.** Lastly, $v_{r,max}$ can only be increased by shortening the chirp repetition interval T_{CR}. To do this, two constraints that the radar board has must be considered. First, an up-ramp must be directly followed by a down-ramp, even though sampling only occurs during the up-ramp interval. Second, a pause of at least 20 µs is needed between consecutive frequency chirps, since every chirp needs to be reprogrammed. With this, a down-chirp duration of 12 µs and a chirp repetition interval of 64 µs (accommodating the needed pause) result in a maximum unambiguously measurable velocity of $v_r = \pm 55\,\mathrm{km\,h^{-1}}$. The top speed allowed in regular city streets in Germany is $50\,\mathrm{km\,h^{-1}}$, therefore relative velocities as high as $100\,\mathrm{km\,h^{-1}}$ can occur on two-way streets. This must be accounted for when selecting the scenarios to be studied in Chapters 4 and 5.

The complete parameters of the radar system are listed in Table 2.1. There are two values given for the frame rate. The higher frame rate is achieved only when using a USB 3.0 interface to transfer the data from the radar board to the computer. If instead the slower $100\,\mathrm{Mbit\,s^{-1}}$ Ethernet interface is used, only the lower rate can be achieved.

Table 2.1: Radar system parameters used throughout this work.

Description	Symbol	Value
Center frequency	f_c	76.5 GHz
Sweep bandwidth	B_{sweep}	1 GHz
Chirp repetition interval	T_{CR}	64 µs
Ramp up-time	T_{up}	32 µs
Ramp down-time	t_{down}	12 µs
Sampling frequency	f_s	10 MHz
Frame rate	f_m	25 Hz, 5 Hz
Samples per chirp	K	320
Number of chirps	L	256
Number of Rx channels	U	8
Range resolution	ΔR_0	0.15 m
Velocity resolution	Δv_r	$0.43\,\mathrm{km\,h^{-1}}$
Azimuth angle resolution	$\Delta\theta$	$\approx 13°$
Max. unambiguous range	$R_{0,max}$	23.85 m
Max. unambiguous velocity	$v_{r,max}$	$\pm 55\,\mathrm{km\,h^{-1}}$

2.7.3 Casing and Radome Design

A radome—portmanteau of radar and dome—is the name given to the structure covering the front of the radar sensor. When mounted on a vehicle, it is essential to protect the sensor from being hit by water or debris. The material and thickness of the radome need to be selected carefully, so that reflections can be avoided and losses can be kept at a minimum.

The simplest structure is given by a single plastic plate. In order to avoid reflections caused by the plastic layer (or at least keep them at a minimum), its thickness must be designed to be resonant. This means that the phase difference induced by the electromagnetic wave traveling through the layer must be equal to π or a multiple thereof. Assuming a non-magnetic medium ($\mu_r = 1$), perpendicular wave incidence and a small loss factor ($\tan\delta \leq 0.1$), the resonant material width d_{res} can be given with enough accuracy by [Pfe10, pp. 50]

$$d_{res} \approx n\frac{\lambda_0}{2\sqrt{\epsilon_r'}} = n\frac{\lambda_s}{2} \qquad \text{with } n = 1, 2 \ldots, \tag{2.52}$$

where ϵ_r' is the real part of the material's complex permittivity $\epsilon_r = \epsilon_r'(1 - \mathrm{j}\tan\delta)$. Equation 2.52 shows, that the resonant width must be equal to half a wavelength in medium λ_s, or multiples thereof.

Polyvinyl chloride (PVC) was selected as the radome's material mainly due to its readily availability. The complex permitivitty of PVC at a frequency of 76.5 GHz is

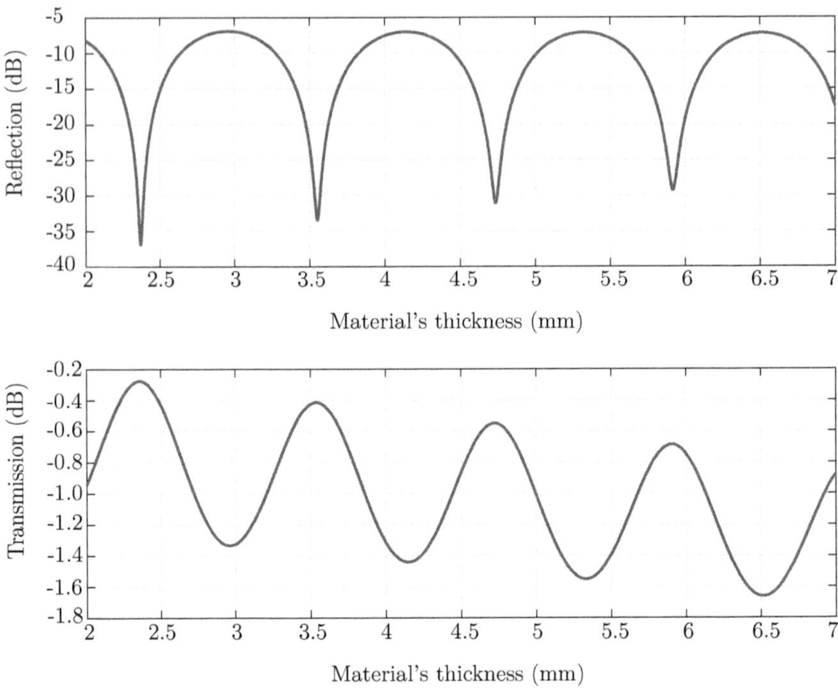

Figure 2.11: One-way transmission and reflection for the vertical polarization and perpendicular wave incidence at $f = 76.5\,\text{GHz}$ as function of the material's thickness.

$\epsilon_{\text{r, PVC}} = 2.74(1 - \text{j}0.009)$ [Fri98, pp. 138], which results in a wavelength in medium of $\lambda_{\text{s,PVC}} = 2.4\,\text{mm}$. Consequently, the resulting resonant widths for the PVC radome are $d_{\text{res,PVC}} \approx n \cdot 1.2\,\text{mm}$. Figure 2.11 depicts the material thickness dependent transmission and reflection coefficients for PVC. For low loss materials, the transmission coefficient is made out of two components: reflection and attenuation in the material (see [Pfe10] for a detailed description of the coefficients). The resonant widths can be seen on the notches of the reflection coefficient, which naturally correspond to the peaks of the transmission coefficient. A thickness of 6 mm is chosen, since it is close to the resonant width of $d_{\text{res,PVC}} = 5.9\,\text{mm}$. This thickness results in a reflection coefficient of $-19.3\,\text{dB}$ and a transmission coefficient of $-0.7\,\text{dB}$ at 76.5 GHz.

The transmission coefficient is subsequently measured across a wide frequency range in order to verify the adequacy of the radome. On the left side of Figure 2.12 the measured transmission through the radome from 65 GHz to 85 GHz is shown. Within the selected operation bandwidth of the radar sensor, the minimum transmission factor

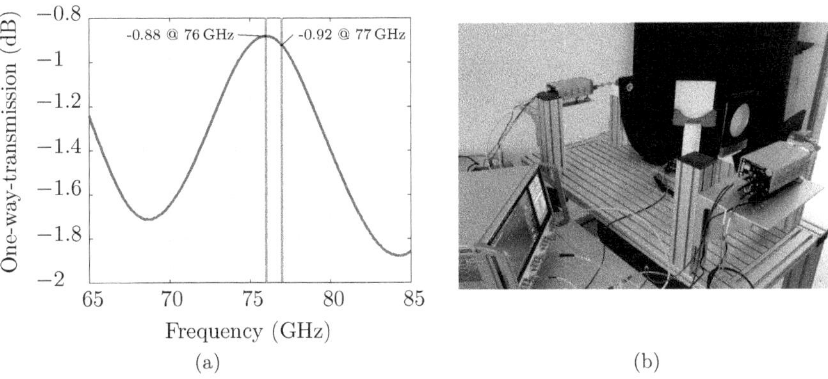

Figure 2.12: One-way-transmission measurement of the PVC radome (a) and the setup used to perform the measurements (b). Picture kindly provided by perisens GmbH.

is −0.92 dB, which is still acceptable for the intended application. Figure 2.12b shows the setup used to perform the transmission measurements (for detailed information refer to [PBS08]).

The rest of the casing is built out of PVC as well for the sake of simplicity. The final enclosure is depicted in Fig. 2.13. As can be seen in Fig. 2.13b, the radome is mounted at an angle of approximately 10°. This is done to deviate any remaining reflections from the main beam direction of the antennas. A ventilator is additionally installed on one of the sides and holes are drilled on the opposite side to allow for air to flow inside the enclosure, which prevents the sensor from overheating.

(a) (b)

Figure 2.13: The *radarbook* evaluation board inside the casing without (a) and with radome (b).

3 Machine Learning Fundamentals

This chapter introduces the fundamental principles of machine learning needed for Chapters 4 and 5. The following derivations are based on the works by Murphy [Mur12], Duda et al. [DHS01] and Patterson et al. [PG17], and are not meant to be exhaustive. For a more detailed insight into deep learning and machine learning in general, the reader is referred to said works.

Broadly speaking, the field of machine learning can be divided into two main categories: supervised and unsupervised learning. With supervised learning, pairs of input-output data are used to infer the function which maps the input to the output. On the other hand, unsupervised learning aims to find structure or patterns in the input data, e.g clustering data points or estimating a probability density function, since no corresponding output data is provided. In this work, the focus is laid on supervised learning. First, general concepts and definitions relevant to supervised learning are introduced. Thereafter, artificial neural networks—starting with the single perceptron and going up to convolutional neural networks—are introduced. Following that, the backpropagation algorithm, which is the backbone of supervised learning, as well as relevant loss and activation functions are presented. Finally, the evaluation metrics used throughout this work are laid out.

3.1 Supervised Learning

The starting point of supervised learning is a labeled dataset, i.e. a set of input values x_i and their corresponding output values, also referred to as labels, y_i. The aim of supervised learning is to estimate the function $g(x)$ which maps the inputs to the outputs:

$$g : x \mapsto y. \tag{3.1}$$

The estimated function $\hat{g}(x)$ can then be used to make predictions $\hat{y} = \hat{g}(x)$ on novel, therefore unseen by the learning algorithm, input values. If y can take on any real-valued number ($y \in \mathbb{R}$), the learning problem is called *regression*. An example of this would be predicting the value of a company stock based on past trends. However, if y may only take a finite number C of values (classes) within a set ($y \in \{0, 1, \ldots C\}$), it is denoted a *classification* problem, e.g. deciding if an image is a picture of a cat or a dog.

The inputs x can be unprocessed data, e.g. the RGB pixel values of an image, or they can also undergo some pre-processing in order to extract only the relevant information. The later process is called feature extraction and it is often desired in order to reduce the dimensions of x and thus reduce the computation time of the learning task.

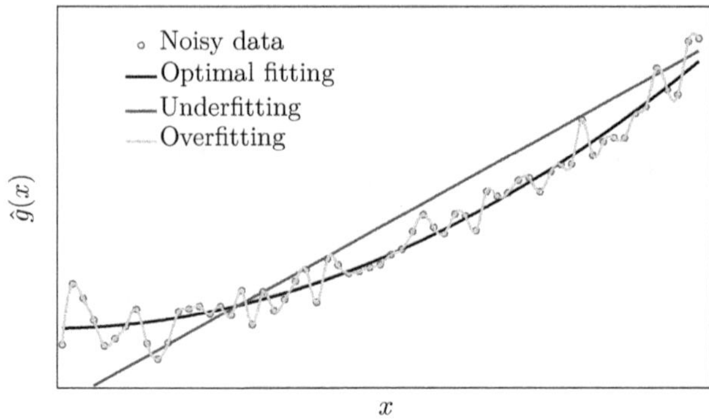

Figure 3.1: Example of an overfitted, an underfitted and an optimally fitted model computed from noisy data.

The ability of a model to accurately predict the output values on unseen input data points is called *generalization*. In order to assess the generalization performance of a model, the dataset is divided in typically three subsets—a *training*, a *validation* and a *test* dataset. The training dataset is used, as the name already suggests, to train the model, i.e. to fit the function to the data. At multiple iterations during the training procedure the performance of the model is evaluated using the validation data set. The process of training and validating can be done iteratively while changing the hyperparameters of the model to improve its performance. Finally, the fine-tuned model is tested with the test dataset. Different models can be compared based on their performance on the test dataset.

A given model may be able to perform exceptionally on the training dataset after a number of training iterations, but still make highly inaccurate predictions when presented with the validation or test datasets. This problem arises when the model is "tightly" fitted to the training data and is therefore known as *overfitting*. The more complexity that is introduced to a model, the more it is able to fit to even small variations in the data. However, these small variations are more likely to be noise than signal and should better be left out of the model [Mur12, pp. 22]. The yellow line in Figure 3.1 portrays an example of an overfitted model.

If the model has on the other hand too few parameters to be able to approximate $g(x)$ accurately, the opposite problem, namely *underfitting*, arises. The purple line in Fig. 3.1 shows a linear model which is not able to fully model the relationship between input and output values of the dataset. This model will not perform well with neither training nor validation data.

Finally, the black line displays what an optimal solution might look like for the predicted function $\hat{g}(x)$. While it does not fit the training data as well as the overfitted model does, it will perform better with previously unseen data.

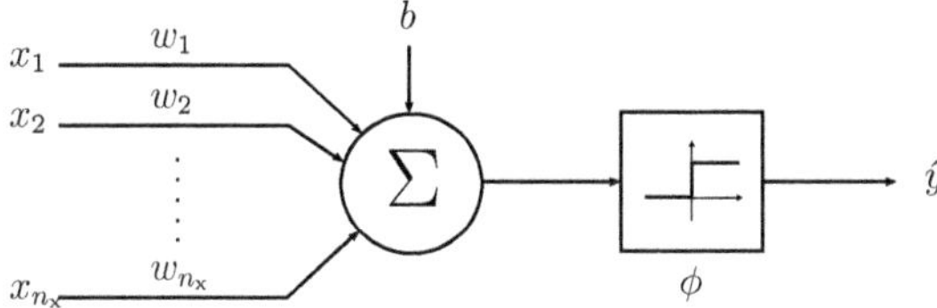

Figure 3.2: A single artificial neuron.

3.2 Artificial Neural Networks

The earliest form of an artificial neural network was introduced by McCulloch and Pitts in 1943 [MP43], where they used a weighted sum of input values and a threshold to mimic biological neural events. However, the artificial neuron as it is known today is more closely related to the *perceptron*—a learning algorithm introduced by Rosenblatt [Ros57, Ros61] to learn the weights and biases (thresholds) of said networks. In this work, the terms perceptron and single artificial neuron will be used interchangeably.

A depiction of the basic structure of an artificial neuron can be seen in Fig. 3.2. It is composed of n_x input values given as an input vector $\boldsymbol{x} = [x_1, x_2, \ldots, x_{n_\mathrm{x}}]^\mathrm{T}$, a weight vector $\boldsymbol{w} = [w_1, w_2, \ldots, w_{n_\mathrm{x}}]^\mathrm{T}$, a bias b, a non-linear activation function ϕ and an output value $\hat{y}$. If the artificial neuron is being compared to the biological neuron, the input vector would correspond to the neuron's *dendrites*, the addition function would be performed by the *soma* and the activation function by the *axon*.

The working principle of the artificial neuron begins with scaling the input values by their corresponding weights and subsequently summing the product with the bias value. The result of this sum then goes trough an activation function—the Heaviside step function in the original definition of the perceptron—and finally, the output value is produced. Mathematically this procedure is expressed as

$$\hat{y} = \phi\left(\sum_{i=1}^{n_\mathrm{x}} w_i \cdot x_i + b\right), \tag{3.2}$$

or using vector notation as

$$\hat{y} = \phi\big(\boldsymbol{w}^\mathrm{T}\boldsymbol{x} + b\big), \tag{3.3}$$

where $\boldsymbol{w}^\mathrm{T}\boldsymbol{x}$ is the matrix product of the transpose of the weight vector $\boldsymbol{w}$ and the input vector $\boldsymbol{x}$. The methods to determine the weights and bias of the network will be discussed in Section 3.3.

A single artificial neuron, as the one pictured in Fig. 3.2, is only capable of implementing linear decision boundaries [DHS01, pp. 289]. Minsky and Papert famously demonstrated this, by proving the inability of the perceptron to implement the exclusive or (XOR) function [MP88]. In order to be able to implement higher order boundaries, multilayer networks are needed.

3.2.1 Multilayer Perceptrons

A multi-layer perceptron (MLP) can be viewed as a series of interconnected neurons, where one neuron's output can be part of the input of another neuron. Figure 3.3 depicts an example of an MLP consisting of an input layer "x" with n_x neurons, a hidden layer "h" with n_h neurons, and an output layer "y" with n_y neurons. Each neuron in the network is represented by a circle and it encompasses the summation unit (including the bias value) and the activation function (see Fig. 3.2).

Analogously to Eq. 3.3, the output of the hidden units $\boldsymbol{h} = [h_1, h_2, \cdots, h_{n_\mathrm{h}}]^\mathrm{T}$ can be computed by

$$\boldsymbol{h} = \Phi\Big(\boldsymbol{W}_\mathrm{xh}^\mathrm{T}\boldsymbol{x} + \boldsymbol{b}_\mathrm{h}\Big), \tag{3.4}$$

where the bias vector $\boldsymbol{b}_\mathrm{h} = [b_1, b_2, \cdots, b_{n_\mathrm{h}}]^\mathrm{T}$ contains the bias values of the hidden layer. Contrary to Equation 3.3, the argument of the activation function is not necessarily a scalar. Therefore, $\Phi(\boldsymbol{z})$ in Equation 3.4, applies element-wise activation functions to the values in $\boldsymbol{z}$. The activation functions at different neurons also do not necessarily have to be the same function. The weight matrix $\boldsymbol{W}_\mathrm{xh}$ in Equation 3.4 is a $n_\mathrm{x} \times n_\mathrm{h}$ matrix with the weights between all neurons in the input and hidden layers:

$$\boldsymbol{W}_\mathrm{xh} = \begin{pmatrix} w_{1,1} & w_{1,2} & \cdots & w_{1,n_\mathrm{h}} \\ w_{2,1} & w_{2,2} & \cdots & w_{2,n_\mathrm{h}} \\ \vdots & \vdots & \ddots & \vdots \\ w_{n_\mathrm{x},1} & w_{n_\mathrm{x},2} & \cdots & w_{n_\mathrm{x},n_\mathrm{h}} \end{pmatrix}. \tag{3.5}$$

Unlike the single perceptron from Fig. 3.2, the MLP depicted in Fig. 3.3 produces multiple output values, which can be grouped under an output vector $\hat{\boldsymbol{y}} = [\hat{y}_1, \hat{y}_2, \ldots, \hat{y}_{n_\mathrm{y}}]^\mathrm{T}$. Defining a corresponding output bias vector $\boldsymbol{b}_\mathrm{y} = [b_1, b_2, \cdots, b_{n_\mathrm{y}}]$ and a $n_\mathrm{h} \times n_\mathrm{y}$ weight matrix $\boldsymbol{W}_\mathrm{hy}$ between the hidden and the output layers, the output of the network can be expressed as

$$\begin{aligned} \hat{\boldsymbol{y}} &= \Phi\Big(\boldsymbol{W}_\mathrm{hy}^\mathrm{T}\boldsymbol{h} + \boldsymbol{b}_\mathrm{y}\Big) \\ &= \Phi\Big(\boldsymbol{W}_\mathrm{hy}^\mathrm{T}\Phi\Big(\boldsymbol{W}_\mathrm{xh}^\mathrm{T}\boldsymbol{x} + \boldsymbol{b}_\mathrm{h}\Big) + \boldsymbol{b}_\mathrm{y}\Big). \end{aligned} \tag{3.6}$$

Equation 3.6 describes the feedforward propagation, also referred as forward pass, of the network. It is one of the two operation modalities of neural networks and it is the one used to perform inference after the weights, biases and other parameters of the network have been determined. The second modality is the training operation, which is responsible for finding the weights and biases of the MLP. In Section 3.3 the backpropagation method for supervised training of neural networks is introduced.

A three layer (input, hidden and output) nonlinear network as the one seen in Fig. 3.3 is capable of representing any arbitrary function, given apt weights and activation functions, and that the hidden layer contains a sufficient number of neurons n_h [DHS01, pp. 287]. It is therefore a so called *universal approximator*.

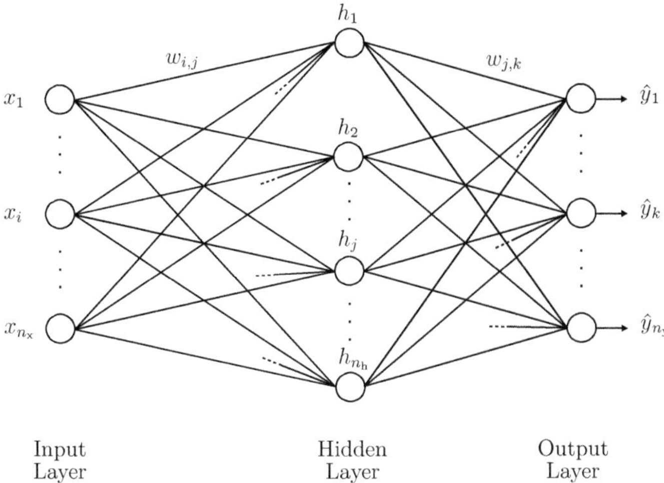

Figure 3.3: Example of a feed forward neural network (multi layer perceptron) with one input layer, one hidden layer and one output layer.

3.2.2 Convolutional Neural Networks

For computer vision tasks, e.g. object detection and classification in RGB images, convolutional neural networks (CNN) have become well-established. They are originally inspired—specifically the convolutional and pooling operations—on the concept of *simple* and *complex* fields, first introduced in a study of the the cat's visual cortex [HW62].

The structure of an exemplary CNN is depicted in Fig. 3.4, which is a common arrangement used for classification tasks. The first part of the network is made out of a series of convolutional and pooling layers with the core idea being, that the convolutional layers extract localized features from the previous layer, which are then merged by the following pooling layer. This procedure can be repeated multiple times to generate a so called feature map. This feature map serves then as the input layer of an MLP, whose layers are denoted *fully-connected layers* due to the fact that each neuron has a weighted connection to every neuron of the following layer.

The working principle of the fully-connected layers has been already discussed in Section 3.2.1. Now, the multi-channel two-dimensional convolution as well as the pooling operations are outlined. Starting with the convolution operation, the input feature map $\boldsymbol{x}$ is a tensor of dimensions $H \times W \times D$. The convolution operation is carried out by sliding a bank of D'' three-dimensional filters $\boldsymbol{f}$ across the first two dimensions of the input feature maps. At each position, the dot product of the filters' weights and the corresponding section of the input map is computed. Additionally, to each filter belongs a bias value specified in the bias vector $\boldsymbol{b}$. The dimensions of all tensors involved in the

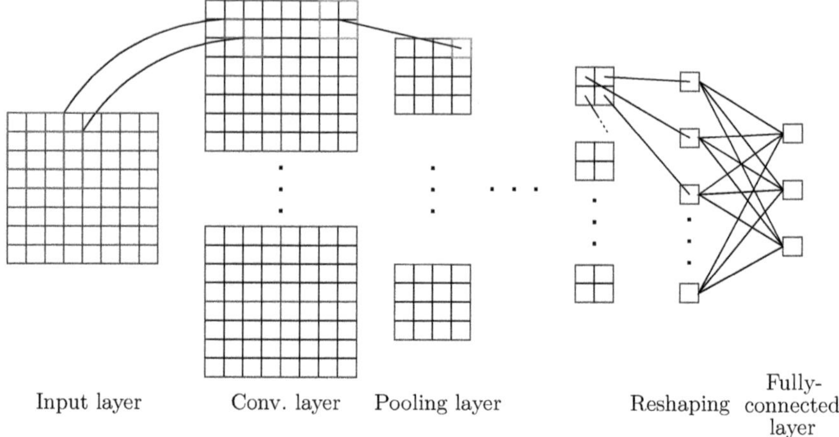

Figure 3.4: Example architecture of a convolutional neural network.

operation are given below:

$$\boldsymbol{x} \in \mathbb{R}^{H \times W \times D}, \quad \boldsymbol{f} \in \mathbb{R}^{H' \times W' \times D \times D''}, \quad \boldsymbol{b} \in \mathbb{R}^{D''}, \quad \boldsymbol{y} \in \mathbb{R}^{H'' \times W'' \times D''}.$$

Formally, the computation of the single values in the output tensor $\boldsymbol{y}$ is expressed as [VL14]

$$y_{i''j''d''} = b_{d''} + \sum_{i'=1}^{H'} \sum_{j'=1}^{W'} \sum_{d'=1}^{D} f_{i'j'd'd''} \cdot x_{i''+i'-1,j''+j'-1,d'}, \tag{3.7}$$

with $i'' = 1, 2 \ldots, H''$, $j'' = 1, 2 \ldots, W''$ and $d'' = 1, 2 \ldots, D''$.

A schematic example of a multi-channel 2D-convolution by one filter can be taken from the left side of Fig. 3.5. One commonly applied technique, that achieves that the height and width of the output map equal the height and width of the input map ($H'' = H$, $W'' = W$), is to pad the edges of the input map with zeros. This procedure is known as *same* padding.

After the convolution operation comes an activation function, which is further addressed in Section 3.4. The subsequent pooling operation combines the information from neighboring fields in the previous layer and by doing so reduces the dimensions of the feature map, achieving some degree of spatial invariance [SMB10]. There are different kinds of pooling filters with the most common ones being *max*-pooling and *average*-pooling. Max-pooling takes the maximum value of each of the d feature channels in a patch of dimensions $H' \times W'$ [VL14]:

$$y_{i''j''d} = \max_{1 \leq i' \leq H', 1 \leq j' \leq W'} x_{i''+i'-1,j''+j'-1,d}. \tag{3.8}$$

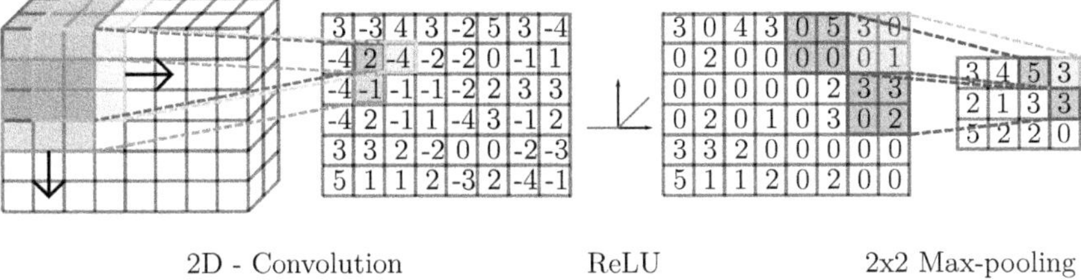

2D - Convolution ReLU 2x2 Max-pooling

Figure 3.5: The three usual operations of a convolutional layer: convolution, activation and pooling. Adapted from [PSRB18].

This results in an output map $\boldsymbol{y} \in \mathbb{R}^{H'' \times W'' \times D}$. As the name already suggests, average-pooling computes the average of the values within the patch:

$$y_{i''j''d} = \frac{1}{W'H'} \sum_{1 \leq i' \leq H', 1 \leq j' \leq W'} x_{i''+i'-1, j''+j'-1, d}, \tag{3.9}$$

which results in an output tensor of the same size as with max-pooling.

3.3 Training of Artificial Neural Networks

In Section 3.2.1 the feed-forward propagation mode of artificial neural networks (ANN) was introduced. It was also mentioned, that with the correct weights, biases and activations an MLP with a hidden layer can approximate any function. Here, the second modality of neural networks, i.e. the one that deals with finding those weights and biases, is presented. This section follows Duda et al. [DHS01, pp. 290-292].

The core principle of training is very simple. First, the network is fed with a training example and it computes a corresponding output value using its current weights and biases. A training error is then calculated based on a pre-defined loss function (see Section 3.5), which reflects the difference between the network's output and the training example's true label. The weights and biases of the network are subsequently updated in a way that reduces the training error. The following derivations show how this is achieved using the *backpropagation* algorithm. They are made for the MLP depicted in Fig. 3.3, however they can also be applied to CNNs and other kinds of ANNs.

The backpropagation algorithm is the backbone of training for most artificial neural networks. It provides the update rule which minimizes the training error—also known as cost—$J(\boldsymbol{w})$. The cost is a function of the weights and biases, which will be both lumped together in a weight vector $\boldsymbol{w}$, since the biases can also be regarded as weights. As an example, the l_2-loss (see Section 3.5) will be used hereafter for the cost function:

$$J(\boldsymbol{w}) = \sum_{k=1}^{n_y} (\hat{y}_k - y_k)^2. \tag{3.10}$$

Since backpropagation is based on gradient descent, the weights are updated following the direction that decreases the training error, i.e. following the negative of the gradient

$$\Delta \boldsymbol{w} = -\eta \frac{\partial J}{\partial \boldsymbol{w}}, \tag{3.11}$$

or for a single weight in the network

$$\Delta w_{p,q} = -\eta \frac{\partial J}{\partial w_{p,q}}, \tag{3.12}$$

where the learning rate η scales the magnitude of the change. To start the training regime, $\boldsymbol{w}$ is initialized with random values. Thereafter, it gets updated iteratively with the change defined in Equation 3.11:

$$\boldsymbol{w}(m+1) = \boldsymbol{w}(m) + \Delta \boldsymbol{w}(m), \tag{3.13}$$

where m indexes the training step.

Going forward, it is helpful to give its own variable to the net activation of a neuron, i.e. the result of the weighted sum before going through the activation function. The net activation α_k of the k-th output neuron is given by

$$\alpha_k = \sum_{j=1}^{n_y} w_{j,k} h_j \tag{3.14}$$

and consequently the value of the k-th output neuron by

$$\hat{y}_k = \phi(\alpha_k). \tag{3.15}$$

Coming back to the 3-layer MLP from Fig. 3.3, first a hidden-to-output weight is considered. In order to calculate the partial derivative of the cost J in relation to the weight $w_{j,k}$, the chain rule for differentiation is needed, since the former does not explicitly depend on the latter:

$$\frac{\partial J}{\partial w_{j,k}} = \frac{\partial J}{\partial \alpha_k} \cdot \frac{\partial \alpha_k}{\partial w_{j,k}} = -\delta_k \frac{\partial \alpha_k}{\partial w_{j,k}}, \tag{3.16}$$

where $\delta_k = -\partial J / \partial \alpha_k$ is introduced to describe how a change on the net activation affects the overall cost and is called the sensitivity of the k-th neuron. Once again the chain rule is applied to compute δ_k:

$$\delta_k = -\frac{\partial J}{\partial \alpha_k} = -\frac{\partial J}{\partial \hat{y}_k} \cdot \frac{\partial \hat{y}_k}{\partial \alpha_k} = 2(y_k - \hat{y}_k) \cdot \phi'(\alpha_k). \tag{3.17}$$

The last equation highlights the importance of differentiability when choosing an activation function. Finally, using Equation 3.14, it can be seen that the rightmost part of Equation 3.16 is simply the output value of the j-th hidden unit:

$$\frac{\partial \alpha_k}{\partial w_{j,k}} = h_j. \tag{3.18}$$

Putting all of this together, the update rule in Equation 3.12 for the hidden-to-output weights becomes

$$\Delta w_{j,k} = \eta \cdot \delta_k \cdot h_j = \eta \cdot 2(y_k - \hat{y}_k) \cdot \phi'(\alpha_k) \cdot h_j. \tag{3.19}$$

Now, the input-to-hidden weights are considered. Analogously to Equation 3.12, the chain rule is applied:

$$\frac{\partial J}{\partial w_{i,j}} = \frac{\partial J}{\partial h_j} \cdot \frac{\partial h_j}{\partial \alpha_j} \cdot \frac{\partial \alpha_j}{\partial w_{i,j}} \tag{3.20}$$

The partial derivative of the cost in regards to the output of the j-th hidden unit (leftmost term on the right side of Equation 3.20) contains all the weights $w_{j,k}$ between that unit and all k output units:

$$\begin{aligned}
\frac{\partial J}{\partial h_j} &= \frac{\partial J}{\partial \hat{y}} \cdot \frac{\partial \hat{y}}{\partial h_j} \\
&= -2\sum_{k=1}^{n_y}(y - \hat{y}) \cdot \frac{\partial \hat{y}}{\partial h_j} \\
&= -2\sum_{k=1}^{n_y}(y - \hat{y}) \cdot \frac{\partial \hat{y}}{\partial \alpha_k} \cdot \frac{\partial \alpha_k}{\partial h_j} \\
&= -2\sum_{k=1}^{n_y}(y - \hat{y}) \cdot \phi'(\alpha_k) \cdot w_{j,k}.
\end{aligned} \tag{3.21}$$

Also in this case, a sensitivity is defined at the j-th hidden unit:

$$\delta_j = \phi'(\alpha_j) \cdot 2\sum_{k=1}^{n_y} w_{j,k}\delta_k \tag{3.22}$$

From Equation 3.22 can be observed, that the sensitivity of a hidden unit is nothing more than the sum of all output units' sensitivities weighted by their respective hidden-to-output weights and then all multiplied by $\phi'(\alpha_j)$. With this, the update rule for the input-to-hidden weights can be expressed as

$$\Delta w_{i,j} = \eta \cdot x_i \cdot \delta_j = \eta \cdot \left[2\sum_{k=1}^{n_y} w_{j,k}\delta_k\right]\phi'(\alpha_j) \cdot x_i \tag{3.23}$$

Equations 3.19 and 3.23 sum up the update rules for the 3 layer ANN which decrease the cost J. The ultimate goal is to minimize the cost function for the whole training dataset, not for a single training example as previously demonstrated. To do that, the cost from Equation 3.10 is computed using the mean loss of all training examples (see Section 3.4). Nonetheless, this can become prohibitively expensive in terms of computing time, when working with deep networks and large amounts of data. A solution for this is to build data batches by randomly sampling the training dataset and using the batch loss to approximate the loss of the whole dataset at every training iteration. This method is known as stochastic gradient descent (SGD).

3.4 Activation Functions

The role of activation functions is to propagate one neuron's output to another neuron in the following layer. They also introduce the nonlinear behavior to the networks. The most commonly used activation functions are plotted in Fig. 3.6 and briefly described below.

- The Heaviside step function is the activation function originally used for Rosenblatt's perceptron. It is a discontinuous function, which is equal to one for positive arguments and zero otherwise:

$$\phi_{\mathrm{H}}(z) = \begin{cases} 1 & \text{if } z > 0 \\ 0 & \text{otherwise} \end{cases}. \tag{3.24}$$

- The logistic function belongs to the family of sigmoid functions. It is often applied when the neurons' values represent probabilities, since its range is the interval $(0, 1)$. It is defined as

$$\phi_{\mathrm{Log}}(z) = \frac{1}{1 + \mathrm{e}^{-z}}. \tag{3.25}$$

- The hyperbolic tangent function is also a member of the sigmoid functions family. This function's range is in the interval of $(-1, 1)$ and is defined as

$$\phi_{\tanh}(z) = \tanh(z) = \frac{\mathrm{e}^{z} - \mathrm{e}^{-z}}{\mathrm{e}^{z} + \mathrm{e}^{-z}}. \tag{3.26}$$

- The rectified linear unit (ReLU) is the most often used activation function in deep learning networks. It is only activated for positive values, where it responds linearly with the input value, otherwise its output value is zero:

$$\phi_{\mathrm{ReLU}}(z) = \max(0, z). \tag{3.27}$$

  It has the advantage of having either a zero, when inactive, or a constant gradient, when active. Therefore, gradient vanishing effects due to nonlinearities, as it is the case with $\phi_{\mathrm{Log}}(z)$ or $\phi_{\tanh}(z)$, will not happen [GBB11].

- The *softmax* activation function is commonly used at the last layer when performing logistic regression for classification purposes, i.e. when $\hat{\boldsymbol{y}}$ stands for a discrete probability density function. This function scales the input values with the exponential function and performs normalization, so that all output values lie within the range $(0, 1)$ and their sum adds up to one. The value of the i-th neuron is given by

$$\phi_{\mathrm{s},i}(\boldsymbol{z}) = \frac{\mathrm{e}^{z_i}}{\sum_{j=1}^{n_y} \mathrm{e}^{z_j}}, \tag{3.28}$$

  with $\boldsymbol{z} = [z_1, z_2, \ldots, z_{n_y}]$.

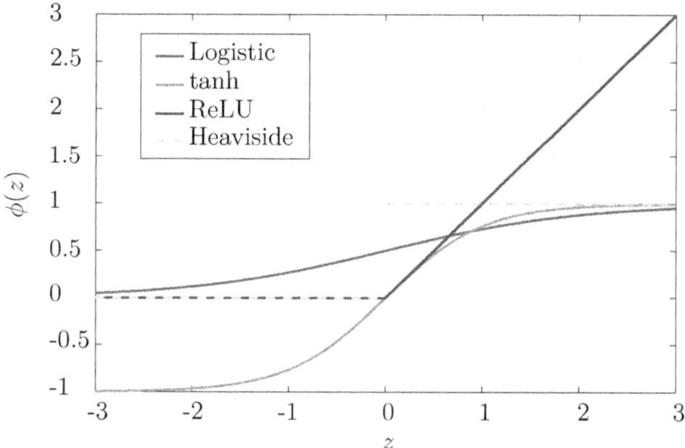

Figure 3.6: Common activation functions.

3.5 Loss Functions

In order for a machine learning algorithm to fit a model to the available data, a function which quantifies how good the predicted values $\hat{y}$ approximate true values y is needed. Such a function is called loss (or cost) function l and it is the starting point of the optimization task. Depending on the specific task, different loss functions can be employed. Below, some of the most common loss functions are introduced.

- For regression problems, a commonly used loss function is the squared error or l_2-loss [Mur12, pp. 178]:
$$l_2 = (\hat{y} - y)^2. \tag{3.29}$$
- The l_2-loss function increases quadratically with the difference between predictions and ground truth data. Consequently, if a data set contains outliers, these would be strongly reflected in the l_2-loss function. For these cases, a less sensible to outliers and thus more robust loss function is presented by the absolute error or l_1-loss [Mur12, pp. 179]:
$$l_1 = |\hat{y} - y|. \tag{3.30}$$
- If the task at hand is a hard classification instead of a regression problem, the hinge loss l_h belongs to the most commonly used ones [PG17]. For the case that $y \in \{-1, 1\}$, the hinge loss is defined as:
$$l_\text{h} = \max(0, 1 - y \cdot \hat{y}). \tag{3.31}$$
- For classification problems it is often not desired to make a hard classification, but to give an estimate of the probability for each of the possible classes instead. This

kind of problem is known as logistic regression. A measure of the dissimilarity between two probability distributions p and q is given by the cross-entropy $H(p, q)$. It can therefore be used as a loss between the true probability distribution y and the estimated distribution $\hat{y}$. The cross-entropy loss l_{XE} is defined as:

$$l_{\text{XE}} = -H(y, \hat{y}) = -y \cdot \log \hat{y}. \tag{3.32}$$

When optimizing a machine learning model, usually the mean over a set of training data points of the loss is used. The mean loss $\bar{l}$ is given by

$$\bar{l} = \frac{1}{N} \sum_{i=1}^{N} l_i, \tag{3.33}$$

where N is the number of examples in the data set and l an arbitrary loss function.

3.6 Evaluation Metrics

Since machine learning can be employed for many different kinds of problems, a universal metric on which to evaluate a model's performance does not exist. Instead, multiple metrics have been established depending on the relevant task. The metrics employed in this work are presented below.

- A *confusion matrix* displays the relationship between true classes and predicted classes in table format. The values therein can either be given in absolute numbers or as a ratio of number of predictions to total number of data samples. If the task at hand is a binary classification, the classes can be viewed as positive (P) or negative (N) examples. The resulting confusion matrix from such a case is presented below.

  Table 3.1: Confusion matrix for a binary classification problem.

	$\hat{y} = P$	$\hat{y} = N$
$y = P$	tp	fn
$y = N$	fp	tn

  In Table 3.1, tp stands for true positives, fp for false positives, fn for false negatives and tn for true negatives. From this terminology, the remaining performance meters can be derived.

- The *accuracy* can be described in general as a measurement of closeness of the predicted values to the true values. In numbers, it is given by

$$a = \frac{\text{tp} + \text{tn}}{\text{tp} + \text{fp} + \text{tn} + \text{fn}}. \tag{3.34}$$

When dealing with imbalanced data sets—e.g. when the positive examples largely outweigh the negative ones—the accuracy is not an appropriate metric, since always predicting the dominant class would provide a high accuracy value without really assessing the real world performance of the model.

- *Precision*, also known as positive predictive value, is a metric that relates the correctly identified members of a class to the overall predicted members of that class:

$$p = \frac{\mathrm{tp}}{\mathrm{tp} + \mathrm{fp}}. \tag{3.35}$$

- The *recall*, or sensitivity, relates the correctly identified members of a class to the overall true number of members in that class:

$$r = \frac{\mathrm{tp}}{\mathrm{tp} + \mathrm{fn}}. \tag{3.36}$$

- Both the precision and recall metrics are dependent on the selected decision threshold. Considering once again the binary classification problem, if the threshold for a positive classification were to be lowered, tp would increase and fn would decrease, achieving a greater recall. Nonetheless, the number of false positives could also grow, effectively lowering the precision. The opposite happens if the threshold is increased. One way to visualize this relationship is by plotting the precision for varying values of recall, which is known as the precision-recall curve.

  Since it is often practical to have a single number to evaluate models, the average precision AP summarizes the shape of the precision-recall curve. It is defined in [EVGW+10] as the mean precision at 11 equidistant recall levels $(0, 0.1, \ldots, 1)$:

$$\mathrm{AP} = \frac{1}{11} \sum_{r \in \{0, 0.1, \ldots, 1\}} p_{\mathrm{interp}}(r). \tag{3.37}$$

  The interpolated precision $p_{\mathrm{interp}}(r)$ is the maximum precision measured at a recall equal or above r:

$$p_{\mathrm{interp}}(r) = \max_{\tilde{r}: \tilde{r} \geq r} p(\tilde{r}). \tag{3.38}$$

  The reasoning behind the interpolation is to reduce the impact of wiggles in the curve [EVGW+10].

  Due to the fact that the AP is class specific, the mean average precision (mAP), which averages the APs of all C classes, is commonly used as well:

$$\mathrm{mAP} = \frac{1}{C} \sum_{i=1}^{C} \mathrm{AP}_i. \tag{3.39}$$

4 Classification of Vulnerable Road Users

This chapter presents two approaches for classifying vulnerable road users using CNNs. First, the micro-Doppler effect, on which both approaches are based, is presented. Following that, the first approach, which classifies whole radar datacubes, is laid out. Lastly, a joint radar and lidar detection and classification system is presented.

4.1 The Micro-Doppler Effect

While doing the derivations of the radar signal model in Chapter 2, it was assumed for the sake of simplicity that persons and objects can be modeled as a single point in space, from which the electromagnetic signal is reflected back to the radar sensor. However, in reality this is not the case, especially when a measurement is performed using a modern radar sensor with high range and velocity resolutions. With this kind of sensor, it is possible to resolve multiple components of a body in motion, e.g. the swinging arms and legs of a pedestrian or the rotating wheels of a car. In such a case, the baseband signal is composed of the superposition of multiple reflection points, all with their own amplitude A_i, frequencies $f_{\mathrm{B},i}$, $f_{\mathrm{D},i}$ and $f_{\theta,i}$, and phase $\phi_{0,i}$. Using Equation 2.44 for the superposition of all reflection points yields:

$$\begin{aligned} s_{\mu\mathrm{D}}(k,l,u) &= \sum_i A_i \cdot s_{\mathrm{B}}(k,l,u)_i \\ &= \sum_i A_i \exp\left(\mathrm{j}2\pi\left(f_{\mathrm{B},i} \cdot \frac{k}{f_{\mathrm{s}}} + f_{\mathrm{D},i} \cdot l \cdot T_{\mathrm{CR}} + f_{\theta,i} \cdot u + \phi_{0,i}\right)\right). \end{aligned} \tag{4.1}$$

The aforementioned extra components appear in the Doppler frequency spectrum as sidebands of the bulk movement's Doppler frequency. This phenomenon is known in the literature as the micro-Doppler effect [Che00].

The micro-Doppler effect has long been of interest for radar target classification, due to the fact that targets can often be characterized by certain motion patterns. Chen et al. first studied and modeled the effect different micro motions, e.g. rotations, vibrations or tumbling, have on radar signals [CLHW06]. This sparked an interest in military and surveillance applications, e.g. to differentiate between tracked vehicles, wheeled vehicles and personnel [SWB06], to classify aircraft types [MEA+14], or to distinguish between different kinds of unmanned aerial vehicles and birds [MHdW+14].

For civilian applications, the micro-Doppler effect in radar has also been thoroughly exploited. Examples of this are hand gesture recognition and motion sensing by the

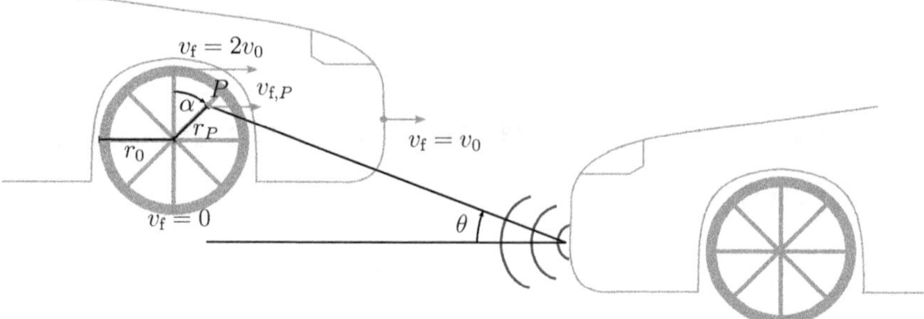

Figure 4.1: Radial velocity of multiple reflection points in a forward moving car.

Google Soli^{TM} project [LGK+16], life signals detection for rescue of earthquake survivors [Nar11], or room occupancy sensing [SUF18]. In the automotive sector, the micro-Doppler effect has most notably been applied to the classification of VRUs. Below, the underlying motions of automobiles, pedestrians and cyclists, as well as their effect on radar signals, are illustrated. These build the basis for the classification systems of the following sections.

4.1.1 Automobiles

Starting with automobiles, there are a number of characteristic points from where radar signals are reflected, e.g. the center of the front or rear end, the corner of the vehicle and the wheelhouses [BB06], [BML+18]. When a car is in motion, the radar range-Doppler signatures caused by the rotating wheels, also observed by Kellner et al. [KBK+15], are especially interesting. To further investigate this, the radial velocity of an arbitrary point on a car's wheel is derived below.

Figure 4.1 exemplarily depicts three points on a car's wheel: the center point of contact with the ground, the topmost point and an arbitrary point P on the wheel's surface. If the car is moving forward at a constant velocity v_f, the top point of the wheel has a velocity component in the forward direction of $v_f = 2v_0$. On the other hand, the bottom part of the tire has—assuming no slipping—a velocity component in the same direction equal to zero ($v_f = 0$). The arbitrarily positioned reflection point on the wheel's surface P will have a forward moving velocity between those values: $v_f \in [0, 2v_f]$. Analytically, $v_{f,P}$ is given by:

$$v_{f,P} = v_0 \cdot \Big(1 + \frac{r_P}{r_0} \cdot \cos(\alpha)\Big), \tag{4.2}$$

where r_0 is the wheel's radius, r_P the distance between P and the center of the wheel, and α the angle between an imaginary line joining the top and center of the wheel, and the point P.

Now, assuming that the car equipped with the radar sensor is stationary, the relative radial velocity between the point P and the radar sensor is given by taking into account the relative heading angle θ:

$$v_{\mathrm{r}P} = v_{\mathrm{f},P} \cdot \cos(\theta) = v_0 \cdot \left(1 + \frac{r_P}{r_0} \cdot \cos(\alpha)\right) \cdot \cos(\theta). \tag{4.3}$$

In this case, the radial velocity falls within the interval $[0, 2v_{\mathrm{f}} \cos(\theta)]$. Nonetheless, measurements have shown that these velocity components are not always present on the range-Doppler spectrum. The probability of measuring a certain velocity is highly dependent on the geometry of the rims and on the visible area of the wheel and thus, on the relative heading angle θ. A horizontal area on the wheel's surface covers only a specific velocity interval, therefore, assuming a solid and uniform geometry of the wheel, the observed velocities follow the distribution

$$v_{\mathrm{r}P} \sim c_\theta \sin\left(\arccos\left(\frac{x}{v \cdot \cos(\theta)}\right) - 1\right) \quad \text{for } x \in [0, 2v_{\mathrm{f}} \cos(\theta)], \tag{4.4}$$

where $c_\theta > 0$ is an integration constant [EPBB20]. Therefore, designing a single-shot rule-based classifier, assuming all the velocity points on the wheels will be observed, is a difficult task.

Figure 4.2 depicts scenes from cars with a slice of the range-Doppler-angle power spectrum on the left and a reference camera picture on the right (refer to Fig. 4.7 for the measurement setup). On the first scenario (Fig. 4.2a), a car driving away from the radar sensor is displayed. The power spectrum shows that the multiple reflection points are spread across both range and velocity dimensions—as expected based on the previous derivations. The reflections coming from the left front and left rear wheels can be clearly observed spanning a wide velocity range, which goes both above and below the bulk velocity component of the car.

The second scenario (Fig. 4.2b) depicts the same car one frame later, i.e. 40 ms later. Although the car has barely moved, a noticeable difference in the micro-Doppler signature of the car can be observed. This can be traced back to the geometry of the wheels' rims, since the position of the spokes changes with the wheels' angular velocity.

The further away the car is from the radar, the smaller the visible area on the wheels becomes and the more the shape of the car approaches a straight line. This would also be the case in a scenario where the car performing the radar measurement is driving directly behind the target car, i.e. for $\theta = 0°$.

The third scenario is displayed in Figure 4.2c. In this case, a car driving in perpendicular direction to the sensor's boresight direction can be seen. The strongest reflection point on the body of the car has a relative radial velocity of zero. However, since the car is crossing near the radar, certain parts of the vehicle still have a radial velocity component in regards to the sensor. This can clearly be observed in the velocity profile on the range-Doppler-angle spectrum. Were the car at the same angle, but further away from the radar sensor, it would appear as a single reflection point with zero radial velocity.

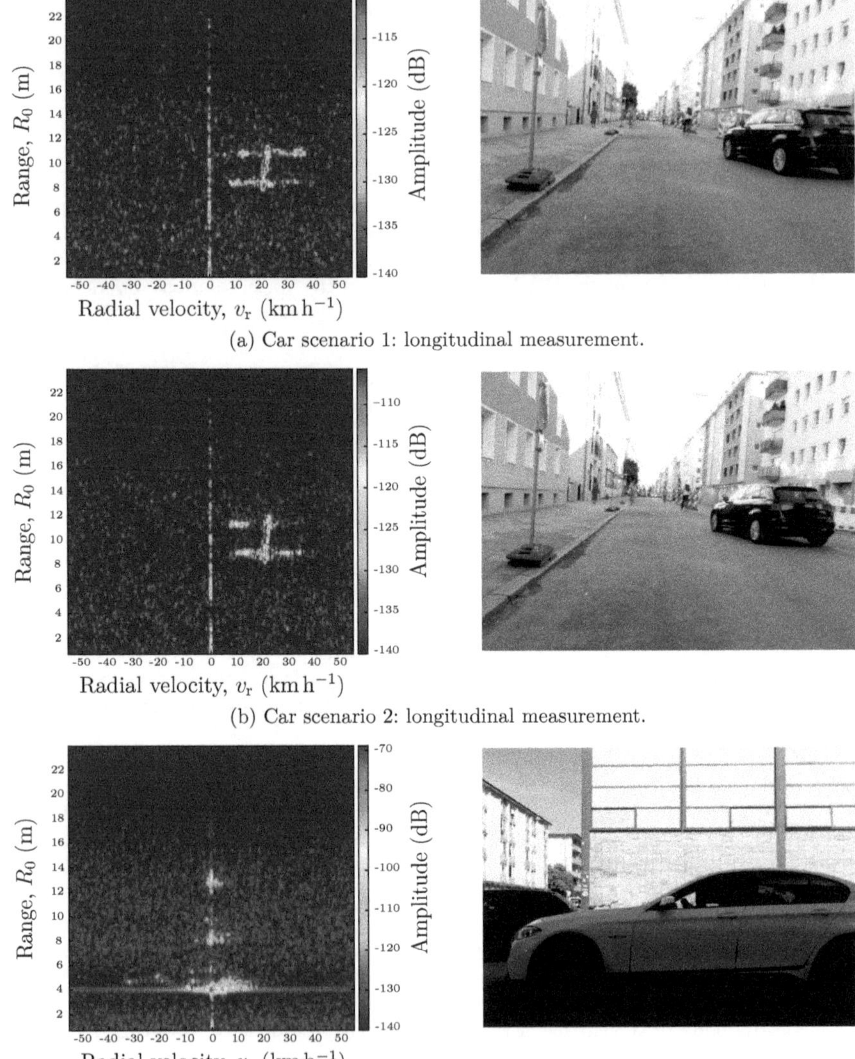

(a) Car scenario 1: longitudinal measurement.

(b) Car scenario 2: longitudinal measurement.

(c) Car scenario 3: lateral measurement.

Figure 4.2: Range-Doppler-angle spectrum at fixed angle bins (left side) and camera picture (right side) of different car scenarios.

4.1.2 Pedestrians

A walking pedestrian can likewise be modeled by a series of reflection points, each with its own relative velocity, distributed across its body. Van Dorp et al. described the walking motion of a person, by dividing them in 12 body parts (modeled as ellipsoids or spheres), 3 translation trajectories and 14 rotation trajectories [vG03]. Using the walking motion model from Boulic et al. [BTT90], the motion of each of the body parts is computed based on three parameters: the cycle frequency, the cycle length and the cycle phase. A cycle is thereby defined to be the time between two contacts of the same heel with the ground.

Since the gait is a periodic motion, it is best observed over a prolonged time period. A commonly found method to achieve this is by applying the short time fast Fourier transform (STFT), with which the periodicity of the micro-Doppler components becomes clearly visible. On the other hand, the range-Doppler-angle spectrum widely used in this work provides only snapshots of these motions at fixed intervals. Nonetheless, below it is demonstrated, that it is also possible to observe features of the micro motions using the range-Doppler-angle power spectrum.

Figure 4.3 portrays three examples of pedestrians walking in front of the radar sensor, with the same arrangement as in Fig. 4.2. In the first scenario (Fig. 4.3a), the pedestrian is illuminated by the radar sensor while walking away longitudinally. The walking person exhibits, due to its small—compared to a car—physical dimensions, a very narrow range profile. Two reflection points in range Dimension are visible in this first scenario: the upper one belongs to the head, while the lower encompasses both the torso and the legs. In the velocity dimension, the pedestrian's profile extends over multiple bins spanning around $10\,\mathrm{km\,h^{-1}}$. In this case, the additional velocity components are caused by the swinging motion of the person's legs. Multiple observations of this effect can also be found in the literature, e.g. [RR07], [VGKN09], or [SMKM15b]. Schubert et al. additionally modeled pedestrians by defining multiple point-shaped reflection centers distributed across the whole body [SKFM14].

The second scenario, depicted in Fig. 4.3b, shows a pedestrian walking laterally in regards to the radar sensor. Since their heading direction and the radar's boresight direction are nearly perpendicular, the relative radial velocity is effectively null. This results in a point-shaped target in both range and Doppler dimensions, as evidently shown in the left side of Fig. 4.3b.

Lastly, Fig. 4.3c depicts the same pedestrian as in the second scenario, but a couple of frames later. As a consequence of the small increase in relative azimuth angle, the relative radial velocity of the bulk movement becomes non-zero. Additionally, micro-Doppler components can be observed on the range-Doppler-angle spectrum. This shows that, even for small angles of incidence, short range measurements of laterally moving pedestrians exhibit some micro-Doppler components. Similar observations can also be found in the works by Bartsch et al. [BFR12] and Schubert et al. [SMKM15b].

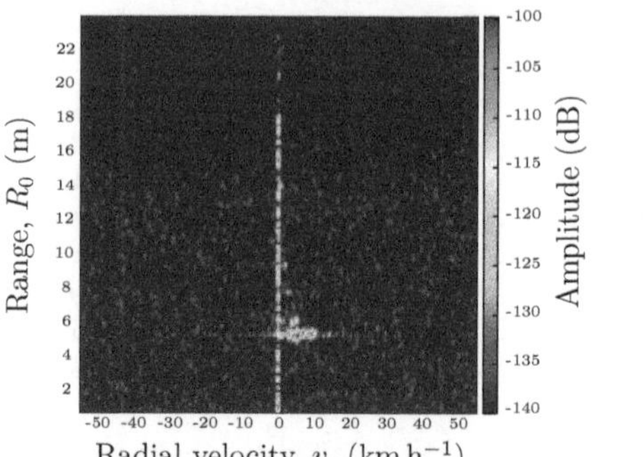

(a) Pedestrian scenario 1: longitudinal measurement.

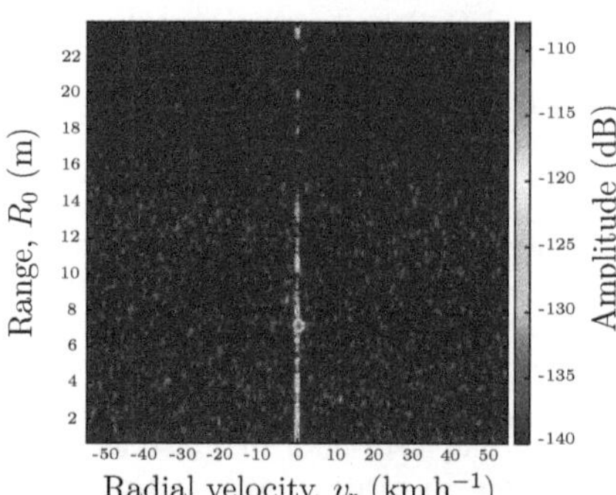

(b) Pedestrian scenario 2: lateral measurement.

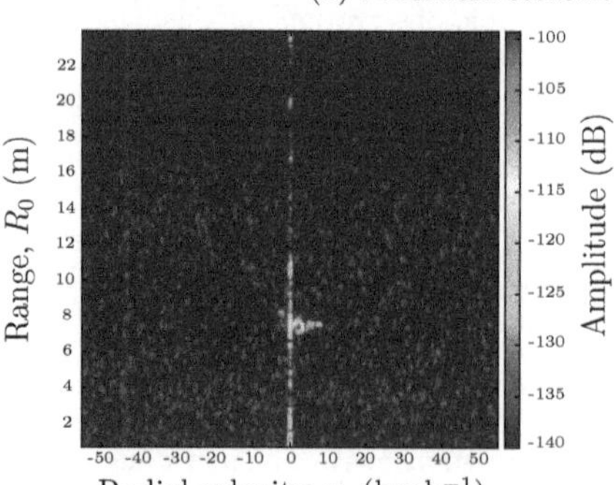

(c) Pedestrian scenario 3: lateral measurement.

Figure 4.3: Range-Doppler-angle spectrum at fixed angle bins (left side) and camera picture (right side) of different pedestrian scenarios.

4.1.3 Cyclists

The last of the road users to be analyzed on the range-Doppler-angle spectrum are cyclists. Figure 4.4 depicts the three cyclist scenarios being considered: two with dominant longitudinal velocity components and one with a dominant lateral component.

In the first scenario (Fig. 4.4a), the cyclist is approaching the radar sensor at a radial velocity of around $23\,\mathrm{km\,h^{-1}}$. The range profile spanning around $1.5\,\mathrm{m}$ shows that reflection points exist across the whole frame and wheels of the bicycle. Regarding the components stemming from reflections on the wheels, the same idea as with the car applies to their radial velocity, namely they lie within the interval $[0, 2v_\mathrm{f}\cos(\theta)]$. Parts from the cyclist's body are clearly visible as well, e.g. one of the legs appears as a strong reflection point at a lower velocity than the velocity of the frame due to the pedaling motion. In contrast to the spokes on a car's wheel, the spokes on a bicycle are usually very thin, which results in a smaller RCS and thus weaker contributions on the spectrum.

Figure 4.4b depicts a cyclist moving away from the radar. In this case, the cyclist is not pedaling and thus the velocity component sideways from the bulk velocity component does not exist. However, since the wheels are still rotating, the reflections on the spokes are clearly visible.

The third and last scenario can be seen in Fig. 4.4c. In this example, the cyclist is crossing near the boresight line of the radar. It appears as a strong, point-like reflection area concentrated at $0\,\mathrm{km\,h^{-1}}$. The area on the spectrum is slightly larger than the one from the lateral pedestrian in Fig. 4.3b.

Similar longitudinal and lateral measurements of cyclists with automotive radars can be also found in the literature, e.g. [PHV+18] and [SMKM15b]. As with the pedestrian case, a multi-point model for cyclists that includes both the bicycle and the cyclist in motion was developed by Schubert et al. [SSM+17].

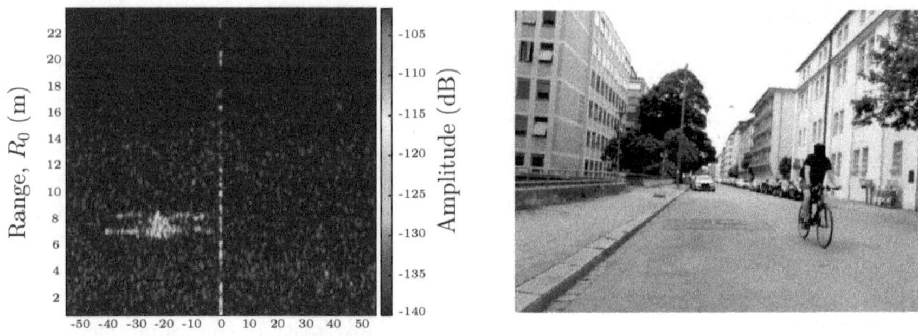

(a) Cyclist scenario 1: longitudinal measurement.

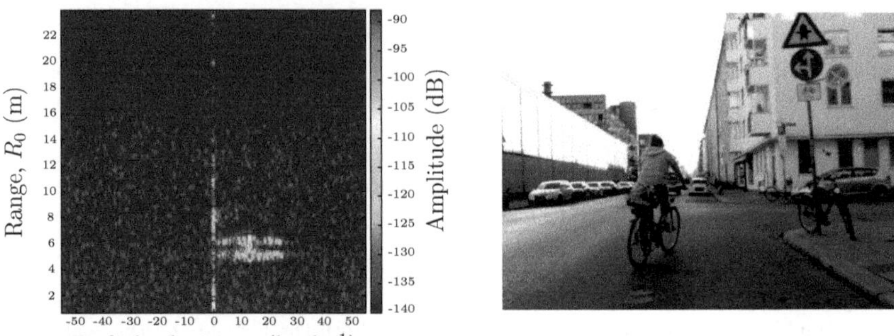

(b) Cyclist scenario 2: longitudinal measurement.

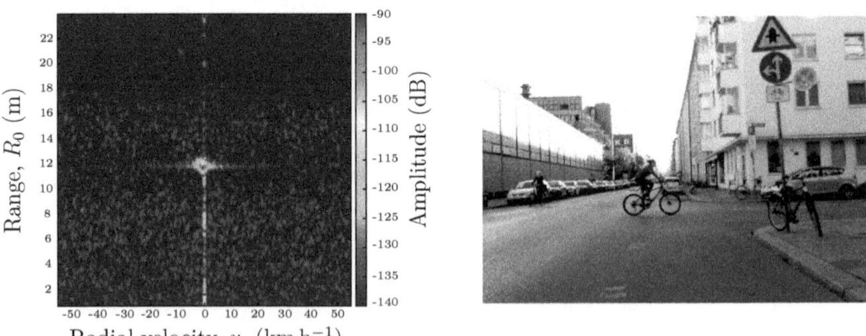

(c) Cyclist scenario 3: lateral measurement.

Figure 4.4: Range-Doppler-angle spectrum at fixed angle bins (left side) and camera picture (right side) of different cyclist scenarios.

4.2 Single Frame Vulnerable Road Users Classification

The last section highlighted some of the main differences that radar measurements of pedestrians, cyclists and cars exhibit. Based on those differences, it is possible to train machine learning algorithms to classify the aforementioned road users in urban scenarios. In this section, a single frame VRUs classification system, previously published in [PSRB18], is presented. It is the first published—to the best of the author's knowledge—system to perform single shot classification with a deep learning approach directly on the raw radar spectrum. First, the related work, including both preceding and succeeding publications, is introduced below.

4.2.1 Related Work

The field of radar target classification in the automotive sector took off in the first decade of the twenty-first century. Earlier works combined radar and vision sensors [MB01] or radar and thermopile sensors [LSMD05]. One of the first classification systems that uses exclusively a radar sensor is based on extracting features from the range profile and Doppler spectrum and, in a later step, feeding them to a polynomial classifier [RHR10]. Later iterations of that system extract features directly from the range-Doppler spectrum and classifies them with a support vector machine (SVM) [HR12]. The used features include among others the extension in range and velocity dimensions and the RCS and are selected by hand. Another similar approach is later presented in [PHV+18], where pedestrians, vehicles, cyclists and dogs are classified with a 79 GHz radar. For this approach, a number of features are extracted from the range-Doppler map and fed into different types of classifiers, such as multiple SVM and k-nearest neighbors (KNN) variations, or into a one-layer fully connected ANN. In a subsequent work, they apply a feature extractor on regions of interest (ROI) of the range-Doppler spectrum and feed these features to different variations of an SVM to classify them as either 'pedestrian' or 'other' [PHO+18].

A different approach opts for using knowledge-based weighting functions on the feature vectors, which are also extracted from the spatial distribution and Doppler spread, to differentiate between pedestrians and static objects [BFR12]. By avoiding machine learning completely, this approach allows for a transparent decision process and thus for gaining insight to the source of misclassified samples.

The alternative to hand-picking the features is to allow a deep learning algorithm to learn them itself. This is the principle of deep learning, e.g. the CNNs introduced in Section 3.2.2. Experiences from the computer vision domain demonstrate that deep learning clearly outperforms traditional computer vision techniques. An example of this is the introduction of the AlexNet [KSH12] for the ImageNet Large Scale Visual Recognition Challenge [RDS+15], which established CNNs as the state of the art solution for image recognition.

This trend of leaving the feature extraction to deep learning also caught up in the domain of radar signal processing, especially for target classification tasks. The core idea of these new approaches is to treat a radar spectrum or map as an optical image.

For example, Kim and Moon applied a deep CNN on spectrograms to identify humans from other targets and to additionally classify their activities, such as running or crawling [KM16]. For human activity classification, Park et al. used a deep CNN on radar spectrograms as well [PJMK16]. Thereby, they used a network pre-trained on the ImageNet dataset, which is a method known as transfer learning. Jokanovic et al. al trained a deep learning algorithm to detect the human fall motion in spectrograms [JAA16].

Deep learning for radar target classification also became increasingly common in automotive applications. However, since the long measurement time needed for the time-frequency analysis (spectrogram) is not viable in this area, other representations of the radar signals are favored. Lombacher et al. apply a CNN to detect arbitrarily parked cars on radar occupancy and amplitude grids [LHDW15]. On a later work they classify static objects such as parked cars, buildings and trees based on radar grids and deep learning as well [LHDW17]. Martínez et al. propose a parking space monitoring system based on slant-range images from a multiple-input multiple-output (MIMO) FMCW radar, which they classify with a CNN as free or occupied [MZV18]. Another work based on classifying radar grid maps is presented by Prophet et al. [PLSV19]. They apply a semantic segmentation network—which assigns a class to each pixel in an image—to classify static objects and structures on multi-channel radar maps (occupancy grid, signal-to-noise ratio (SNR) grid, and height map).

The first published work—as far as can be confirmed by a thorough literature search—to classify road users with a deep learning approach directly on the raw range-Doppler-angle spectrum is [PSRB18], which is the one presented in Section 4.2.2. The main contribution from this system is that it demonstrates that it is possible to classify road users on the raw frequency spectrum using a single radar measurement. Succeeding publications from other research groups also adapt a similar approach. For example, Patel et al. propose a system to classify static urban targets by extracting regions of interest from the range-azimuth spectrum and feeding them through a CNN [PRV+19]. Palffy et al. combine low-level (a 3-dimensional crop of the range-Doppler-angle (RDA) spectrum) with target-level values (detected range, velocity, angle and RCS) to classify VRUs [PDKG20].

An approach usually applied to lidar point clouds is presented by Schumann et al. [SHDW18]. They employ a modified version of PointNet(++) [QYSG17] to perform semantic segmentation on four-dimensional (two spatial coordinates, the compensated radial velocity and the RCS) radar point clouds. While this approach has the advantage of both avoiding the hand-selection of features as well as the clustering procedure, it still relies on the CFAR detection procedure, which might discard valuable information.

4.2.2 System Concept

The aim of this system is to study the feasibility of performing single shot classifications based solely on radar measurements. Therefore, simple measurement scenarios, where only one moving target is present, are contemplated. The overall classification procedure is depicted in Fig. 4.5.

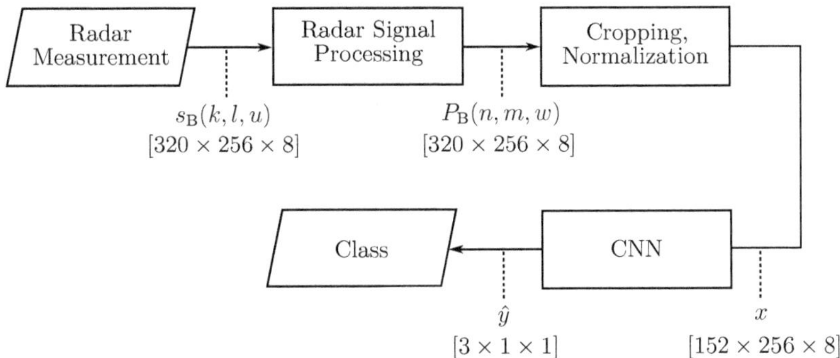

Figure 4.5: The overall process from radar measurement to classification. Adapted from [PSRB18].

a) **Radar measurement.** A single chirp sequence FMCW radar measurement is sampled 320 times during each of the 256 frequency ramp at each of the 8 receive channels, which produces a three-dimensional data array of size $[320 \times 256 \times 8]$. The details of the radar system's and waveform's configurations can be taken from Table 2.1. Since the USB interface is used for this system, a measurement rate of $f_{\mathrm{m}} = 25\,\mathrm{Hz}$ is achieved.

b) **Radar signal processing.** This block computes the range-Doppler-angle power spectrum $P_{\mathrm{B}}(n, m, w)$ as per Equation 2.46. However, some additional signal processing procedures are necessary to prepare the signal. First, a Hann window is applied to the first two dimensions (samples and chirps) of the time-domain signal in order to suppress the side-lobes in the frequency domain. In the case of the receiver dimension, no window is applied to avoid widening of the main lobe. All FFTs are computed without using zero-padding.

When computing the FFT across the receive channels, it is assumed that they are sampled simultaneously. However, as already mentioned in Section 2.7.2, the receive channels in the *radarbook* are sampled sequentially. This introduces a beat frequency dependent phase shift, whose slope increases with the time lag [Inr15a]. Since the time lag is known (inverse proportional to the sampling frequency of the ADC), this can be easily corrected after the first FFT by multiplying the range spectrum with an array containing the corresponding phase shifts.

c) **Cropping and normalization.** The *radarbook* does not have an I/Q mixer and thus its output consists of only real-valued signals. Since the Fourier transform of real-valued signals produces a Hermitian frequency spectrum, half of the values—i.e. the ones corresponding to positive beat frequencies—provide no additional information and can thus be discarded.

A well-known effect of FMCW radar is the cross-talk between transmit and receive paths. This leads to a high zero-frequency component, which renders the first couple of range bins useless. For this reason, the RDA power spectrum is cropped, leaving out all bins corresponding to a range smaller than 1 m. After cropping, the resulting data array has the dimensions [152 × 256 × 8]. Following that, the cropped RDA power spectrum is converted to decibels:

$$P_{\mathrm{B,dB}} = 10 \cdot \log_{10}(P_{\mathrm{B}})\,\mathrm{dB}. \tag{4.5}$$

In order to facilitate the learning procedure, the input data is normalized to have zero-mean and a small standard deviation of 0.5. The input signal of the CNN is then given by

$$x = \frac{0.5}{\sigma_{\mathrm{P}}} \cdot (P_{\mathrm{B,dB}} - \mu_{\mathrm{P}}), \tag{4.6}$$

where σ_{P} is the standard deviation and μ_{P} the mean of the RDA power spectrum.

d) **Convolutional neural network.** The network architecture of the CNN is depicted in Fig. 4.6. It is inspired by the architecture from Kim and Moon [KM16], which classifies human activity based on radar spectrograms. It is made out of 2 convolutional and two fully-connected layers. At the input, the normalized spectrum x is interpreted as an 8 channel image, where the channel dimension is the azimuth angle dimension. The convolution filters are slid across the first two dimensions, i.e. the range and radial velocity dimensions. After every convolution operation comes a rectified linear unit (ReLU) as activation function followed by a pooling operation, which reduces the dimensions of the feature maps. For the pooling operation, max-pooling is chosen and it operates across the first 2 dimensions as well. At the end of the second convolutional layer, the feature map is reshaped into a one-dimensional array. A ReLU follows the first fully-connected layer, while a softmax function follows the last layer in order to convert the output logits into the predicted probability distribution $\hat{y}$. The specific details about the size and number of filters at each layer, as well as the overall data flow across the network, can be taken from Table 4.1.

e) **Classification.** The CNN assigns a probability prediction to each one of the three classes and the class with the highest probability is selected. This procedure is evaluated for each measurement frame individually.

4.2.3 Dataset

The dataset is gathered by performing measurements on multiple urban street locations in the area surrounding the main campus of the Technical University of Munich. The radar sensor is mounted on a wagon as pictured in Fig. 4.7. A webcam is brought on on top of the radar casing, in order to aid the labeling process. For each radar measurement frame, a snapshot is taken and assigned to it. Figure 4.8 displays multiple camera pictures in some of the measurement locations. As can bee seen from Fig. 4.8, the measurements contain subjects moving in longitudinal as well as in lateral direction with regards to the radar sensor's boresight.

The presented classification system is able to make only one single prediction per radar datacube. Therefore, the algorithm relies on having only one single moving target present at any radar measurement frame. To facilitate this, the start of a measurement series

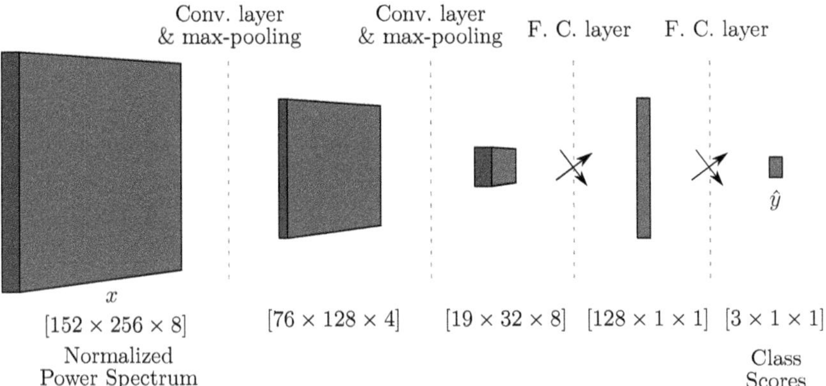

Figure 4.6: Convolutional neural network architecture for classifying VRUs as pedestrians, bicycles or cars based on the RDA power spectrum. Adapted from [PSRB18].

Table 4.1: Detailed structure of the convolutional neural network in Fig. 4.6. Adapted from [PSRB18].

Layer	Type	Input size	Filter size	Nr. of filters	Output size
1	Convolutional	$152 \times 256 \times 8$	$5 \times 5 \times 8$	4	$152 \times 256 \times 4$
	ReLU	$76 \times 128 \times 4$	-	-	$76 \times 128 \times 4$
	Max-pooling	$152 \times 256 \times 4$	$2 \times 2 \times 1$	-	$76 \times 128 \times 4$
2	Convolutional	$76 \times 128 \times 4$	$5 \times 5 \times 4$	8	$76 \times 128 \times 8$
	ReLU	$76 \times 128 \times 8$	-	-	$76 \times 128 \times 8$
	Max-pooling	$76 \times 128 \times 8$	$4 \times 4 \times 1$	-	$19 \times 32 \times 8$
	Reshaping	$19 \times 32 \times 8$	-	-	$4864 \times 1 \times 1$
3	Fully-connected	$4864 \times 1 \times 1$	-	-	$128 \times 1 \times 1$
	ReLu	$128 \times 1 \times 1$	-	-	$128 \times 1 \times 1$
4	Fully-connected	$128 \times 1 \times 1$	-	-	$3 \times 1 \times 1$
	Softmax	$3 \times 1 \times 1$	-	-	$3 \times 1 \times 1$

Figure 4.7: Measurement setup. The *radarbook* is placed on a measurement wagon at a street crossing. The webcam on top provides reference pictures to each radar frame. Source: [PSRB18].

is triggered manually when single-target scenarios arise. However, radar frames with multiple targets are inevitably also recorded. For this reason, the dataset is controlled by hand using self-developed MATLAB GUI, which is also used to assign a class to each measurement frame.

The resulting datasets are laid out in Table 4.2. Multiple measurement frames belonging to the same subject are referred to as a track. Training and test datasets contain different tracks, in order to reduce the correlation between datasets. The tracks in the training and test dataset 1 (Tables 4.3a and 4.3b) are from measurements which share the same street locations. On the other hand, the test dataset 2 is recorded on different street locations to further evaluate the generalization capabilities of the approach.

4.2.4 Training

The convolutional neural network is implemented using the Tensorflow software library [AAB+15]. Training is performed on a MacBook Pro with a 2.7 GHz Quad-Core Intel Core i7 Processor for about 35 epochs, which took approximately 4 hours. To update the weights the SGD optimizer with a learning rate of $\eta = 0.05$ is applied. Since this is purely a logistic regression problem, the cross entropy loss function l_{XE} from Equation 3.32 is selected.

To forestall overfitting, a technique called *dropout* [SHK+14] is applied during training. Dropout severs the connection between two neurons randomly with a probability of p. This prevents the network from putting too much weight on single neurons and, instead, forces it to focus on the combination of multiple neurons, which favors its generalization

Figure 4.8: Example webcam pictures from the training data set. Source: [PSRB18]

Table 4.2: Distribution of training and test datasets. Test set 1 contains tracks not used during training, but which are gathered in the same street locations as tracks from the training set. Test set 2 contains tracks from unseen street locations during training.

(a) Training set.

Class	Tracks	Frames
Ped.	50	3396
Cyclist	92	3394
Car	49	2347

(b) Test set 1.

Class	Tracks	Frames
Ped.	6	301
Cyclist	7	301
Car	8	294

(c) Test set 2.

Class	Tracks	Frames
Ped.	5	221
Cyclist	4	194
Car	4	126

capabilities. A dropout probability of $p = 0.4$ is used during the training procedure.

4.2.5 Results and Evaluation

The classification results computed with the test set from Table 4.3b are laid out in the confusion matrix in Table 4.4. The classification system correctly classifies all pedestrian frames. More problematic are in this case the cyclist and car tracks. The cyclist frames get wrongfully classified as pedestrians 0.3% of the time and as cars 2% of the time. For the car frames, 0.7% get classified as pedestrians and 5.1% as cars. The overall accuracy, as defined in Equation 3.34, for this test set is $a = 0.97$.

Table 4.5 shows the confusion matrix computed with the data from the second test dataset (Table 4.3c). When compared to the first data set, a general decrease in the accuracy can be observed. For this specific set, the accuracy drops to $a = 0.84$. A

Table 4.4: Confusion matrix computed with test set 1 (Table 4.3b)

		Predicted class		
		Pedestrian (%)	Cyclist (%)	Car (%)
True class	Pedestrian	100	0	0
	Cyclist	0.3	97.7	2.0
	Car	0.7	5.1	94.2

Table 4.5: Confusion matrix computed with test set 2 (Table 4.3c)

		Predicted class		
		Pedestrian (%)	Cyclist (%)	Car (%)
True class	Pedestrian	91.4	5.0	3.6
	Cyclist	2.0	68.6	29.4
	Car	0	4.0	96.0

performance diminution is especially found for the cyclist class, which only gets correctly classified for 68.6% of all frames.

The worsened performance of the second test set highlights the need of a large and heterogeneous dataset for training and evaluating the system. Since for this approach the whole radar datacube is given as an input, it is evident that the change in scenery, i.e. the addition and removal of static objects, is enough to confuse the network. While this system shows that single-shot classification is possible, the achieved performance is not enough for urban automotive scenarios. For that, the dataset would have to be expanded considerably.

4.3 Joint Lidar and Radar Classification System

The system presented in the last section demonstrated that single-shot classification based solely on the radar range-Doppler-angle spectrum is possible. However, such a system is only capable of classifying single-target scenarios. This limitation prevents it from being viable in automotive scenarios, where multiple targets can be present at any given time. Therefore, another approach, which performs a detection beforehand, is necessary. In this section, the joint lidar and radar classification system, first introduced in [PSRB19a], is presented.

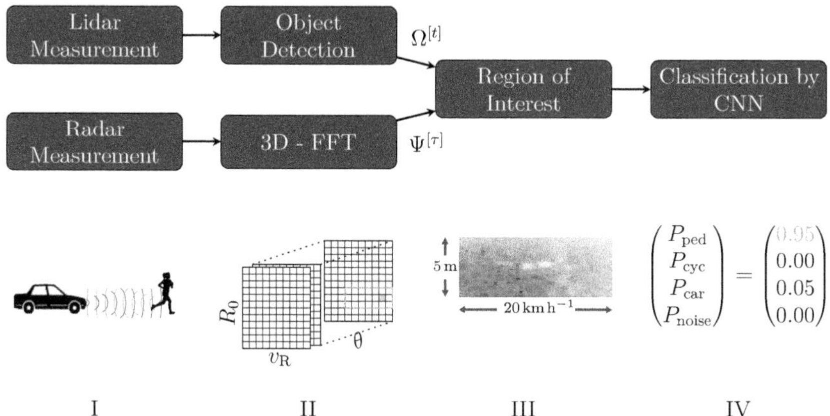

Figure 4.9: Description of the joint lidar and radar classification system. At stage I, both radar and lidar measurements are performed (asynchronous). Stage II provides the lidar object list $\Omega^{(t)}$ and the processed radar measurement $\Psi^{(\tau)}$, which contains the range-Doppler-angle power spectrum. Using the timestamps, the measurements are matched at stage III and the ROIs are extracted from the power spectrum. At stage IV, the ROIs are classified by the CNN. Adapted from [PSRB19a].

4.3.1 System Concept

The overall detection and classification procedure is depicted in Fig. 4.9. It uses a lidar sensor to detect objects in the surroundings of the vehicle and the radar sensor to classify these objects. It would of course also be possible to do both detection and classification exclusively with the radar sensor. However, detection and tracking algorithms would have to be developed and implemented. Since the test vehicle already provides a reliable detection and tracking system with the lidar sensor and the focus of the work is laid on the classification of vulnerable road users, it is decided in favor of using the lidar sensor for this task.

a) **Radar measurement.** The radar system parameters are the same as in the system from Section 4.2 and can be taken from Table 2.1. However, in order for the radar sensor to work with the measurement framework within the test vehicle, the 100 Mbit s^{-1} Ethernet interface has to be used and therefore a measurement frequency of only $f_m = 5$ Hz is possible.

b) **Radar signal processing.** The same signal processing steps are taken as in Section 4.2 to compute the RDA power spectrum $P_{B,dB}$. However, for this system the angle FFT is computed with a length of 16 by padding the signals with zeros. This is done to achieve a finer granularity of the angle regions, which is helpful when cutting an ROI out of the radar datacube. The radar signal processing block produces at each discrete time step τ the tupel

$$\Psi^{[\tau]} = \left\{ P_{\mathrm{B}}{}^{[\tau]}, \mathrm{ts}^{[\tau]} \right\}, \tag{4.7}$$

where ts is the time-stamp of the radar measurement.

c) **Lidar measurement.** The lidar operates at a measurement frequency of around 25 Hz. At each discrete time step t, it produces an object list denoted $\Omega^{[t]}$. The k-th object $O_k^{[t]}$ within $\Omega^{[t]}$ is a tupel

$$O_k^{[t]} = \left\{ \mathrm{id}_k^{[t]}, \mathrm{ts}_k^{[t]}, x_k^{[t]}, y_k^{[t]}, v_{x,k}^{[t]}, v_{y,k}^{[t]} \right\}, \tag{4.8}$$

where id_k is an identification number given to the k-th object and ts_k the time-stamp of the measurement. The lidar sensor predicts a bounding box for every object and the position of its center point in the vehicle's coordinate system is given by x_k and y_k. In the same manner, the object's velocity components in x and y direction are given by the values $v_{x,k}$ and $v_{y,k}$. These are predicted through the sensor's tracking algorithm, due to the fact that a lidar cannot measure the velocity directly.

d) **Region of Interest.** Since the lidar and radar measurements are not initiated by a common source, the measurements must be matched to one another using their respective time stamps. The radar measurement frequency f_{m} is lower than the lidar's and thus for each radar measurement a lidar measurement that best matches the radar's time stamp is selected. Therefore, from here on the discrete radar measurement index τ is used to index both radar and lidar measurements.

Having built a radar-lidar measurement pair, all the objects on the lidar object list $\Omega^{[\tau]}$—excluding those outside of the radar's FOV—are mapped to a location within the RDA power spectrum. This is done by transforming an object's spatial coordinates (x_k and y_k) into a range $R_{0,k}$ and azimuth angle θ_k inside the radar's coordinate system. Analogously, the object's radial velocity component $v_{\mathrm{r},k}$ is obtained from the velocity components in x and y direction.

The ROI is a two-dimensional window (in range and velocity dimensions) of the RDA power spectrum P_{B} centered at $(R_{0,k}, v_{\mathrm{r},k}, \theta_k)$. Since the locations at P_{B} are discrete in nature, the values provided by the lidar are usually somewhere in between two bins. Therefore, the locations are simply assigned to the bins that are the closest to them. The resulting ROI has a rectangular form and a fixed size of $5\,\mathrm{m} \times 20\,\mathrm{km\,h^{-1}}$ (see Fig.4.9 - III). This size is chosen in order to fit the range and micro-Doppler signatures of most targets observed in the dataset, while keeping it as small as possible and therefore avoid getting part of neighboring objects' signatures inside the ROI.

e) **Classification by CNN.** The ROIs are pre-processed before going into the CNN by subtracting their mean and scaling them to have a standard deviation of 0.5. The architecture of the convolutional neural network is depicted in Fig. 4.10. It is inspired by the VGGNet architecture by Simonyan and Zisserman [SZ14]. Instead of going the classical way of following a convolution operation with a ReLU and a pooling operation, a convolutional and a ReLU layer are directly followed by another convolutional and ReLU layer and then by a pooling layer.

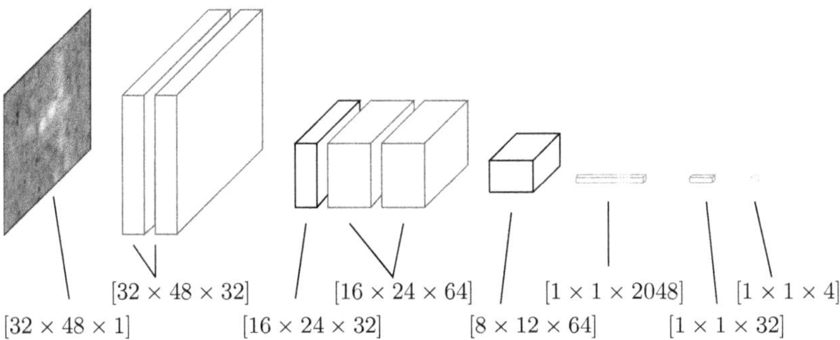

Figure 4.10: Convolutional neural network architecture based on VGGNet [SZ14]. Adapted from [PSRB19a].

A more detailed structure of the classification network is given in Table 4.6. All convolution filters have a receptive field's size of 3×3 in the first two dimensions. Max-pooling is the operation chosen to reduce the dimensionality of the feature maps. After the last fully-connected layer, the softmax activation function computes the predicted probability density function $\boldsymbol{p} = [P_{\text{ped}}, P_{\text{cyc}}, P_{\text{car}}, P_{\text{noise}}]$, where P_{ped} is the probability of the ROI containing a pedestrian, P_{cyc} a cyclist, P_{car} a car, and P_{noise} no target, i.e. it contains just background noise. The class with the highest probability is then assigned to the ROI.

4.3.2 Data Acquisition

In order to create a more realistic dataset than the one in Section 4.2, the data for this system is gathered by driving with a test vehicle in the inner city of Munich. For this purpose, a BMW 5 Series (F10) equipped with a variety of surround and inertial sensors is used. The more relevant sensors for this work (camera, lidar and radar) are highlighted in Fig. 4.11. The radar system is fitted within the right kidney grill using the enclosure described in Section 2.7.3. The camera, which is mounted in place of the rear-view mirror, is solely used as an aid during the labeling process. The sensors are coupled to an on-board computer through the robot operating system (ROS) framework. The ROS-nodes of each sensor provide measurement time-stamps, which are used to match them to each other, as explained in Section 4.3.

The dataset is created by a semi-automatic labeling process, since the lidar sensor already provides a class prediction additionally to the object's position and velocity. Nonetheless, the class and position of the ROI must be checked and corrected manually when necessary. Due to the fact that the classification system predicts only one class

Table 4.6: Detailed structure of the convolutional neural network in Fig. 4.10.

Layer	Type	Input size	Filter size	Nr. of filters	Output size
1	Convolutional	$32 \times 48 \times 1$	$3 \times 3 \times 1$	32	$32 \times 48 \times 32$
	ReLU	$32 \times 48 \times 32$	-	-	$32 \times 48 \times 32$
2	Convolutional	$32 \times 48 \times 32$	$3 \times 3 \times 32$	32	$32 \times 48 \times 32$
	ReLU	$32 \times 48 \times 32$	-	-	$32 \times 48 \times 32$
	Max-pooling	$32 \times 48 \times 32$	$2 \times 2 \times 1$	-	$16 \times 24 \times 32$
3	Convolutional	$16 \times 24 \times 32$	$3 \times 3 \times 32$	64	$16 \times 24 \times 64$
	ReLU	$16 \times 24 \times 64$	-	-	$16 \times 24 \times 64$
4	Convolutional	$16 \times 24 \times 64$	$3 \times 3 \times 64$	64	$16 \times 24 \times 64$
	ReLU	$16 \times 24 \times 64$	-	-	$16 \times 24 \times 64$
	Max-pooling	$16 \times 24 \times 64$	$2 \times 2 \times 1$	-	$8 \times 12 \times 64$
	Reshaping	$8 \times 12 \times 64$	-	-	$1 \times 1 \times 2048$
5	Fully-connected	$1 \times 1 \times 2048$	-	-	$1 \times 1 \times 32$
	ReLU	$1 \times 1 \times 32$	-	-	$1 \times 1 \times 32$
6	Fully-connected	$1 \times 1 \times 4$	-	-	$1 \times 1 \times 4$
	Softmax	$1 \times 1 \times 4$	-	-	$1 \times 1 \times 4$

Figure 4.11: Test vehicle (BMW 5 Series F10) equipped with radar, lidar and camera sensors. Source: [PSRB19a].

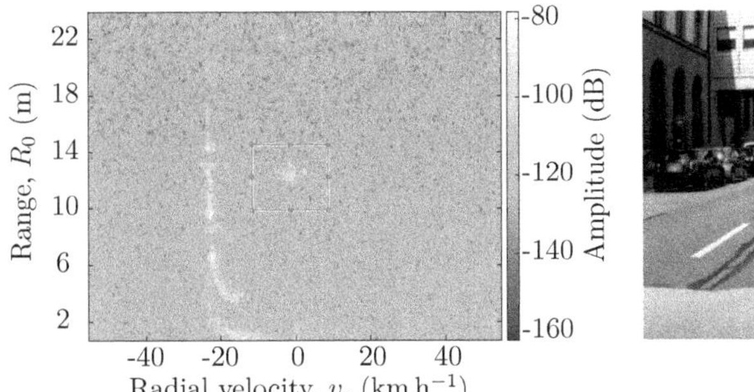

Figure 4.12: Example of a measurement frame with a cyclist in the radar's FOV. The left side shows the range-Doppler-angle power spectrum at a fixed angle bin with the ROI, later used for classification, marked in a red rectangle. The front camera picture is shown on the right side for reference. Adapted from [PSRB19a].

per ROI, solely tracks with one target present or with a clear dominant target within the ROI are selected. Tracks and frames that do not meet this criteria are discarded.

Figure 4.12 depicts an exemplary scenario from the dataset. The ROI belonging to a cyclist is enclosed by the red rectangle on the RDA power spectrum. The cyclist can be seen in front of the ego-vehicle in the camera picture. The blue vehicle further away is not within the maximum range of the radar and thus outside of its FOV.

The distribution from the resulting dataset can be seen in Table 4.7. The train and test sets contain frames from separate tracks. The second test set (Table 4.8c) contains data recorded with the same setup on a different test-vehicle. This dataset has been published and can be retrieved from [PB20].

A measurement track contains an arbitrary number Z of frames belonging to the same object. They are grouped over time by its ID number id_k:

$$T_k = \left\{O_k^{[0]}, O_k^{[1]}, \dots O_k^{[Z]}\right\}. \tag{4.9}$$

The noise tracks are created by manually sampling regions of the range-Doppler-angle power spectrum where no targets are present. The car class includes both small vehicles, such as passenger cars, as well as larger vehicles, such as vans and buses.

4.3.3 Training

The classification network is implemented in TensorFlow [AAB+15]. Same as for the network in Section 4.2, the cross-entropy loss l_{XE} is used. In this case, the Adam optimizer [KB14] is used instead of SGD. Given that the chosen architecture is not very deep, the ROIs are quite small and the convolution filters have a small receptive field, the training phase takes only around 2 minutes. The hardware used for this is

Table 4.7: Distribution of the training and test datasets. Data available from [PB20].

(a) Training set.

Class	Tracks	Frames
Ped.	51	740
Cyclist	80	1943
Car	150	2616
Noise	83	1473

(b) Test set 1.

Class	Tracks	Frames
Ped.	14	264
Cyclist	21	746
Car	62	1834
Noise	17	388

(c) Test set 2.

Class	Tracks	Frames
Ped.	13	276
Cyclist	29	592
Car	70	1234
Noise	27	744

an NVIDIA GeForce GTX 1080 Ti GPU. The time to perform one classification on this hardware during test time, i.e. only the computing time for the CNN excluding all radar signal processing and data pre-processing, is 2 ms.

4.3.4 Evaluation

The classification results using the first test set (Table 4.8b) are laid out in the confusion matrix in Table 4.9 and the class specific precision and recall can be seen in Table 4.10. From both precision and recall metrics can be seen, that the performance for the pedestrian class is the lowest. More insight into the misclassifications is provided by the confusion matrix, where it can be seen that they are often erroneously marked as cyclists and cars. This effect can be explained by the fact that since pedestrians have low radial velocities, the ROIs often also contain static targets, such as parked cars, street poles, etc. The precision of the cyclist class is at 0.82 substantially higher than that of the pedestrian class. However, the recall value is comparably low at 0.62. The confusion matrix shows, that around one third of all cyclist frames are misclassified as cars. For the car class, its recall is quite good at 0.92, while its precision is somewhat lower since, as already discussed, examples of the other 2 classes are often classified as cars. Lastly, the noise class has little errors with both the precision and the recall metrics being near 1.

A closer look into the distribution of the missclassified frames reveals, that errors occur mostly for only a couple of frames within a track. Figure 4.13 depicts the frequency of the relative number of misclassified frames within a track. Tracks that do not contain errors are not included in the graphic. From the histogram it can be observed that tracks with a lower percentage of erroneously classified frames—i.e. the left side—are more frequent than tracks with a high percentage of errors—i.e the right side. This means that aggregating the classifications of ROIs over time could improve the overall classification accuracy by smoothing out the outliers. This is implemented in Section 4.3.5.

Nonetheless, there are still a total of 15 tracks (out of 114), where a majority of the frames are erroneously classified. In a handful of these tracks (5 out of 15), multiple subjects are present inside the ROI. During the labeling process, this kind of occurrence is allowed if it is believed that the subject of interest is still dominant or visible enough.

Table 4.9: Confusion matrix computed with test set 1 (Table 4.8b). Adapted from [PSRB19a].

		Predicted class			
		Pedestrian (%)	Cyclist (%)	Car (%)	Noise (%)
True class	Pedestrian	57.6	15.5	23.9	3.0
	Cyclist	7.0	61.7	30.4	0.9
	Car	3.0	3.1	93.3	0.5
	Noise	0.0	0.0	0.0	100.0

Table 4.10: Class specific precision and recall computed for test set 1 (Table 4.8b). Adapted from [PSRB19a].

	Pedestrian	Cyclist	Car	Noise
p	0.59	0.82	0.86	0.94
r	0.58	0.62	0.93	1.00

Such a scenario is depicted in Fig. 4.14, where two cyclists are riding closely to each other. For the majority of its existence, this track gets falsely classified as a car. The elongated range signature present in the ROI, which is more characteristic of a car, could be one reason for this to happen. Similar scenarios are present in the other tracks, e.g. a group of pedestrians crossing the street or a pedestrian walking at a low velocity near parked cars. This scenarios highlight a weakness of the approach: multiple subjects inside the ROI. The network is not able to correctly identify them, since the training dataset contains mostly ROIs with one single target.

4.3.5 Decision Aggregation

As previously mentioned, filtering the classifications over time could improve the overall accuracy of the system, since many tracks show only a low percentage of misclassified frames. For the task of decision aggregation, a filter that recursively computes the class probabilities is needed and to fulfill this requirement a discrete Bayes filter (DBF) is chosen.

A detected object is modeled as a random state variable X and the four classes are the states x_c that X may take on. The role of the DBF is to recursively estimate at time τ the discrete probability density function

$$\{p_{c,\tau}\} = \{p(X = x_c | z_{1:\tau})\}, \quad c = 1 \ldots 4 \tag{4.10}$$

by assigning a probability $p_{c,\tau}$ to each of the single states based on the measurements

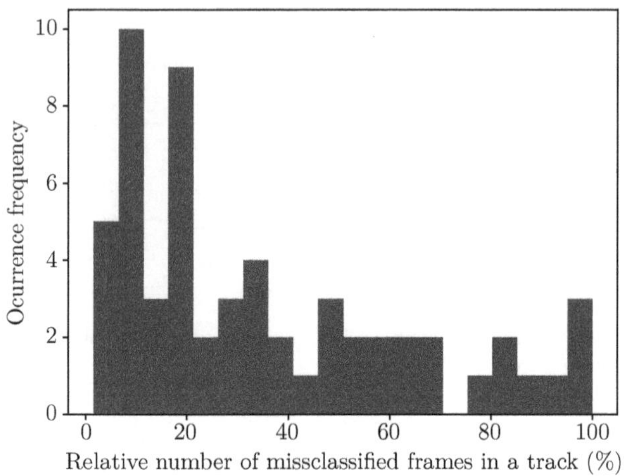

Figure 4.13: Histogram of the relative number of misclassified frames in a track for the test dataset 1 (Table 4.8b). Adapted from [PSRB19a].

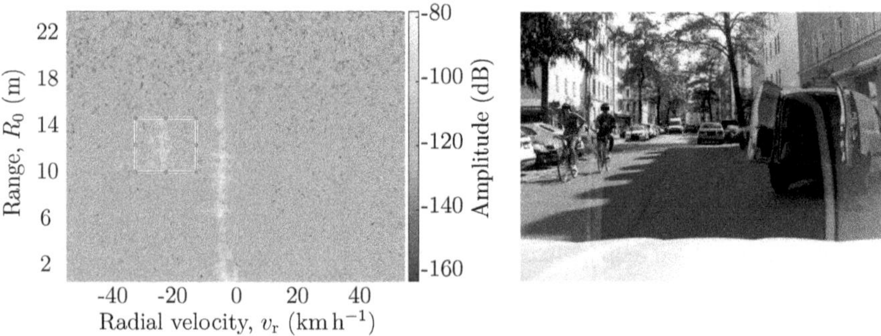

Figure 4.14: A frame taken from test set 1 (Table 4.8b), which contains two cyclists inside the ROI. Adapted from [PSRB19a].

Algorithm 1 Discrete Bayes filter. Adapted from Thrun et al. [TBFA05].

Input: $\{p_{c,\tau-1}\}, z_\tau$

1: **for all** c **do**

2: $\quad \bar{p}_{c,\tau} = \sum_i p(X_\tau = x_c | X_{\tau-1} = x_i)\ p_{i,\tau-1} = p_{c,\tau-1}$

3: $\quad p_{c,\tau} = \eta\ p(z_\tau | X_\tau = x_c)\ \bar{p}_{c,\tau}$

4: **end for**

5: **return** $\{p_{c,\tau}\}$

$z_{1:\tau}$ up to the time point τ. The measurement z is in this case the selected class by the CNN, i.e. the class with the highest probability.

The working principle of the DBF is described in Algorithm 1. For each detected object $O_k^{[\tau]}$ at measurement time τ, the algorithm loops over all four states (classes) and computes their respective probability $p_{c,\tau}$. In order to do this, the so called prediction $\bar{p}_{c,\tau}$, also known as prior, is first calculated in Line 2. This is done by multiplying the class's probability at the previous time step $p_{i,\tau-1}$ with the state transition probability $p(X_\tau = x_c | X_{\tau-1} = x_i)$, which represents the probability of going from state x_i at time $\tau - 1$ to the state x_c at time τ. In this implementation, it is assumed that an object should not change class during its existence as a track. For this reason it follows that the prior is equal to the previous class probability, i.e.

$$p(X_\tau = x_c | X_{\tau-1} = x_i) = \begin{cases} 1, & \text{if } x_c = x_i \\ 0, & \text{otherwise} \end{cases} \tag{4.11}$$

and therefore $\bar{p}_{c,\tau} = p_{c,\tau-1}$. Line 3 of the algorithm incorporates the current measurement z_τ by means of its likelihood function $p(z_\tau | X_\tau = x_c)$. The likelihood functions are derived from the statistics provided by the confusion matrix in Table 4.9. For example, pedestrians get classified by the CNN as pedestrians 57.6% and as cyclists 15.5% of the time, consequently the likelihoods are $p(z_\tau = \text{“pedestrian”} | X_\tau = \text{“pedestrian”}) = 0.576$ and $p(z_\tau = \text{“cyclist”} | X_\tau = \text{“pedestrian”}) = 0.155$. Since the product of the prior and the likelihood function in Line 3 is usually not a probability, a normalization factor η makes sure that all class probabilities $p_{c,\tau}$ add up to one and, thus, that $\{p_{c,\tau}\}$ is a probability density function. For the first frame in a track, the DBF algorithm requires an initial probability density function $\{p_{c,\tau=0}\}$ to calculate the first estimate. The no-knowledge approach, i.e. a uniform distribution, is selected.

The results from aggregating the classifications over time with the DBF can be seen in the confusion matrix from Table 4.11 and in the precision and recall metrics from Table 4.12. From the confusion matrix, a clear improvement in the accuracy of all classes can be observed. Especially, the pedestrian class improves by almost 30%. While the precision of the pedestrian class decreases by a small account, its recall and the cyclist class's recall are significantly improved.

A histogram of the relative number of misclassified frames per track is also created for the approach with the DBF and can be seen in Fig. 4.15. The expected effects can be observed: tracks with a low percentage of errors have even less errors and tracks with

Table 4.11: Confusion matrix computed with test set 1 (Table 4.8b) and applying the DBF. Adapted from [PSRB19a].

		Predicted class			
		Pedestrian (%)	Cyclist (%)	Car (%)	Noise (%)
True class	Pedestrian	84.8	1.9	13.3	0.0
	Cyclist	14.7	81.8	3.1	0.4
	Car	3.6	2.2	94.2	0.0
	Noise	0.0	0.0	0.0	100.0

Table 4.12: Class specific precision and recall computed for test set 1 (Table 4.8b) and applying the DBF. Adapted from [PSRB19a].

	Pedestrian	Cyclist	Car	Noise
p	0.56	0.93	0.97	0.99
r	0.85	0.82	0.94	1.00

a high percentage of errors have even more errors when compared to the histogram in Fig. 4.13. Especially an increase of the tracks with 100% error rate can be observed. However, as seen on the evaluation metrics, an overall performance improvement is achieved.

Due to the fact that the measurement likelihood function $p(z_\tau|X_\tau = x_c)$ in Line 3 of Algorithm 1 is derived from the statistics obtained from the test dataset 1 (Table 4.8b), a different set of data is needed to validate the approach and thus make sure that it does not only work for that specific set. For this purpose the test dataset 2 from Table 4.8c is used. The classification results with and without applying the DBF can be taken from the confusion matrices in Table 4.13 and the precision and recall metrics from Table 4.14. For this dataset too, an improvement for almost all classes can be observed. The accuracy of the car class gets slightly reduced after applying the DBF, but the pedestrian and cyclist classes are improved by a more significant amount.

When compared to the first classification system presented in Section 4.2, this system does not perform as well. There are a couple of differences that attribute to this. First, in contrast to the system in Section 4.2, this system does not take all angle bin channels as input. As a consequence, spatial information gets lost for large targets, e.g. lateral cars and bicycles. Another big difference is the scenarios contained in the dataset, especially for the pedestrian class which is the one that shows the largest drop in accuracy. The datasets of the first system have mostly clear measurements of pedestrians walking on the sidewalk with few obstructions near them. The radar system is also positioned near the sidewalk. However, the datasets used for this system are gathered with the radar

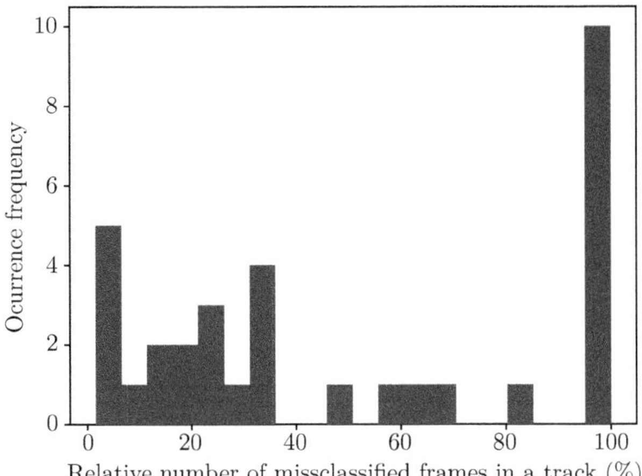

Figure 4.15: Histogram of the relative number of misclassified frames in a track for the test dataset 1 (Table 4.8b). Adapted from [PSRB19a].

Table 4.13: Confusion matrix computed with test set 2 (Table 4.8c) with and without DBF. Adapted from [PSRB19a].

		Predicted class			
		Pedestrian (%)	Cyclist (%)	Car (%)	Noise (%)
	Without DBF				
True class	Pedestrian	65.6	23.2	11.2	0.0
	Cyclist	4.7	85.1	8.6	1.5
	Car	2.1	4.1	93.8	0.0
	Noise	0.0	0.0	0.0	100.0
	With DBF				
True class	Pedestrian	88.4	10.9	0.7	0.0
	Cyclist	5.2	90.0	4.1	0.7
	Car	3.2	3.7	93.0	0.0
	Noise	0.0	0.0	0.0	100.0

Table 4.14: Class specific precision and recall computed for test set 2 (Table 4.8c) with and without the DBF.

	Pedestrian	Cyclist	Car	Noise
Without DBF				
p	0.77	0.81	0.94	1.00
r	0.66	0.85	0.94	0.99
With DBF				
p	0.77	0.87	0.98	0.99
r	0.88	0.90	0.93	1.00

integrated in the test vehicle. The recorded pedestrians are usually illuminated by the radar sensor at a greater angle thus reducing their radial velocity so that their velocity profile overlaps with static objects. Additionally, they are often found near objects with high RCS, such as parked vehicles, metal poles, etc.

4.4 Concluding Remarks

Both systems presented in this chapter perform classification of pedestrians, cyclists and cars using convolutional neural networks. The base for these approaches is the so called micro-Doppler effect, which is shown to exhibit characteristic profiles even when the subject's radial velocity is small, e.g. when a pedestrian is crossing the street. While previous approaches found in the literature use long measurements to create a spectrogram, these systems work on single radar frames consisting of a sequence of chirps, which are much shorter in duration and therefore more viable for urban automotive scenarios.

The main contribution of the first system, which works on the radar data layer L_1 (see Fig. 1.1), is that it demonstrates that it is possible to classify pedestrians, cyclists and cars based on single-frame radar measurements using the range-Doppler-angle power spectrum. The classical approach for automotive radar sensors is to perform a classification once an object track has been established (Layer L_4 in Fig. 1.1), which happens after multiple subsequent detections of the same object. Thus, a system using a similar approach to the one presented here would enable future ADAS to recognize a dangerous situation, e.g. a pedestrian starting to cross the street, in a timely manner. This is an important requirement to achieve fully autonomous vehicles.

For the first system, only simple, single-target scenarios, where the ego-vehicle is stationary, are considered. Under these conditions, a test accuracy as high as $a = 0.97$ is achieved on a test set gathered in the same locations as the training set. Nonetheless, when tested on different street locations, the overall accuracy drops to $a = 0.84$. This effect highlights the importance of gathering a large, heterogeneous dataset for both training and testing of the system. A further limitation of this system is that, since no detection procedure is implemented, only single-target scenarios, where the test subject is clearly a dominant component on the range-Doppler-angle spectrum, can be considered.

The aim of the second system presented in this work is to provide the ability of classifying multiple targets within one measurement frame and to additionally test it in more realistic urban scenarios by gathering the data with test drives in the city. In this case the input for the CNN is an ROI, found through a previous detection procedure (here the Lidar sensor is used). The ROI spans across the range and Doppler dimensions of the range-Doppler-angle spectrum and has a fixed size. This ends up being one of its weaknesses, since multiple targets can fall into the ROI and give rise to classification errors. A tight window around the subject of interest would be in this case beneficial, which is the aim of the system presented in Section 5.1.

The second approach has an overall worse performance than the first system, in great part due to the more complex scenarios being considered. This is observed especially with the pedestrian class, where subjects are often captured at low velocities near strong reflectors, such as parked cars. Another probable cause of the worsened performance is that the objects' angle profile information contained in the RDA spectrum is being left out by only having a 2-dimensional window. Here, expanding the ROI to a 3-dimensional window would be very likely to improve the accuracy.

A clear improvement in the classification performance of the second system is achieved by aggregating classifications over time with a DBF. It would make sense to implement the decision aggregation directly into the deep learning algorithm, e.g. by using recurrent neural networks.

5 Deep Learning Based Radar Target Detection

Both systems presented in Chapter 4 focus solely on the classification of vulnerable road users. In this chapter, the detection task with deep learning approaches is investigated. Two different approaches are presented in the following sections: one based on data layer L_1—i.e. the frequency-domain baseband signal—and one based on data layer L_0—i.e. the raw time-domain baseband signal.

5.1 Detection in Frequency Domain

The difference between object detection and classification is that the former not only provides a category for an object, but also a location within the given image. Traditionally, the object detection pipeline is divided into three separate steps: informative region selection, feature extraction and classification [ZZXW19]. The first step is responsible for selecting areas that may contain an object. While sliding a scalable window across the whole image can cover all cases, it is computationally expensive and therefore selecting a fixed set of templates is a more feasible solution. Next, hand selected features that semantically represent the regions of interest are extracted. Finally, these features are fed to a classifier, e.g. to an SVM.

As with the image classification problem, deep learning models have proven to perform better than traditional approaches for object detection, since their deeper architectures make it possible to learn more complex features [ZZXW19]. A generic deep learning object detection task has the goal of predicting rectangular bounding boxes for all objects in an image and their respective class probabilities. For this purpose there are two main categories of detectors: region proposal-based networks and regression/classification-based networks (also referred to as *single-shot* detectors). The former type of detector consists of a two-step process, namely making object region proposals and assigning a class score to each one of them. An example out of this category is the faster R-CNN network [RHGS15]. On the other hand, single-shot detectors use one single network to perform class predictions on multiple (several-thousand) predefined bounding boxes. This results in them being faster than region proposal-based approaches with the downside of being less accurate. An example of a single-shot detector is the You Only Look Once (YOLO) object detector [RF18].

The usual detection algorithm for radar signals in the automotive industry is CFAR detection or some kind of variation thereof. While some variations better adapt to extended targets, e.g. OS-CFAR, they still have to be parametrized for different scenarios.

After detecting multiple points, a clustering process assigns a number of detection points to an object. However, these clustering methods also have to be parameterized, e.g. having global parameters for the minimum number of points within a defined distance to form clusters stemming from differently sized road users [SMKM15a].

The system laid out in the following section is a novel approach that performs both tasks—i.e. detecting and clustering—simultaneously and additionally provides a class prediction. It was first published in [PSRB19b]. As previously mentioned in Chapter 4, a classification occurs in the usual automotive radar signal processing chain only after having detected an object multiple times. This system, on the other hand, is able to detect and classify small objects, such as pedestrians, as well as large objects, such as cars, using a single radar measurement frame. Before going into details of the system in Section 5.1.2, the related work is discussed below.

5.1.1 Related Work

While the classification of VRUs with deep learning methods is being studied by a handful of research groups (see related work in Section 4.2), the detection part of the radar signal processing chain is still mainly performed with the aforementioned classic methods. However, first attempts at deep learning radar object detection can already be found. For example, Wang et al. detect simulated point targets by sliding a CNN across the range-Doppler spectrum and the network predicts at each position whether a target is present or not [WTL19]. A YOLO-based approach where targets are detected in the range-angle (azimuth) spectrum is presented by Kim et al. [KCK+20]. By choosing this representation, detected objects can be directly positioned in the ego vehicle's coordinate system. Nonetheless, their dataset is not gathered in real streets, a limited number of test subjects is used and the considered scenarios don't include frames with multiple subjects from different classes.

Another similar approach to the one presented in this work is proposed by Sligar [Sli20]. They create a synthetic radar dataset using a physics-based electromagnetic simulation and train a YOLO system to perform detection on the range-Doppler spectrum. Since the data is generated synthetically, the ground truth labels (bounding boxes) can automatically be provided as well. As will be discussed in Section 5.1.4, this is a quite difficult and time consuming task, especially when working on the range-Doppler representation. However, creating a realistic dataset is also a very complex task, e.g. the author of [Sli20] does not include micro-Doppler components, which are an essential part of radar signals, at least in short range scenarios.

Major et al. propose a vehicle detection system in highway scenarios, which operates on the RDA spectrum [MFA+19]. Their model extracts features directly from the 3D datacube, incorporates temporal information with long short-term memory (LSTM) cells and provides bird's eye view detections and velocity estimations with an mAP as high as 88%.

For military applications, a YOLO-based detection system is presented in [ZWCD19]. The authors propose a modified, lightweight version of YOLO and achieve a high mAP detecting three undisclosed type of targets on the radar range-Doppler spectrum.

Table 5.1: Lengths of the range (N), velocity (M) and angle (V) FFTs and resulting dimension of the cropped power spectrum. Adapted from [PSRB19b].

	N	M	V	$\dim(P_{\mathrm{B,max}})$
Configuration I	320	256	16	155×256
Configuration II	1024	512	16	499×512

5.1.2 System Concept

An overview of the deep learning radar object detection system is depicted in Fig. 5.1. The single components of the signal processing chain are outlined below.

a) **Radar measurement.** The same radar system configuration as in Section 4.3 is employed, which means that every measurement frame produces a data array with the dimension $[320 \times 256 \times 8]$. All waveform parameters and radar system configurations can be retrieved from Table 2.1.

b) **Radar signal processing.** The range-Doppler-angle power spectrum in decibels $P_{\mathrm{B,dB}}$ is computed analogously to Sections 4.3 and 4.2. The FFTs are computed using two set of lengths leading to two different system configurations, which are compared later on. The lengths of the N-point range, M-point velocity and V-point angle FFTs can be taken from Table 5.1.

c) **Data pre-processing.** Only distances greater than 1 m are considered and therefore the RDA power spectrum is first cropped. Since the YOLO system expects a two-dimensional image as an input and $P_{\mathrm{B,dB}}$ is a three-dimensional array, the power spectrum is flattened by applying a maximum function across the angle dimension:

$$P_{\mathrm{B,max}} = P_{\mathrm{B,dB}}\Big(n, m, v = v_{max}(n, m)\Big) \tag{5.1}$$

with

$$v_{\mathrm{max}}(n, m) = \arg\max_{v} P_{\mathrm{B,dB}}(n, m, v). \tag{5.2}$$

By flattening the radar datacube, the angle information is effectively lost. It would therefore be possible to only use the range-Doppler spectrum instead and spare the extra computing time of the third FFT. However, it is decided to still use all receive channels and perform the third FFT in order to retain the resulting signal processing gain, which leads to an overall better detection performance.

Lastly, the flattened spectrum $P_{\mathrm{B,max}}$ is scaled and rounded to integer values between 0 and 255, in order to appear as a gray scale image to the YOLO framework.

d) **YOLO radar object detection.** The You Only Look Once object detection system predicts bounding box confidence scores for the objects present in the radar measurement. If the score surpasses a threshold of 0.25, the bounding boxes are drawn on the image, otherwise they are discarded. A more detailed overview of the YOLO system is given in the next section.

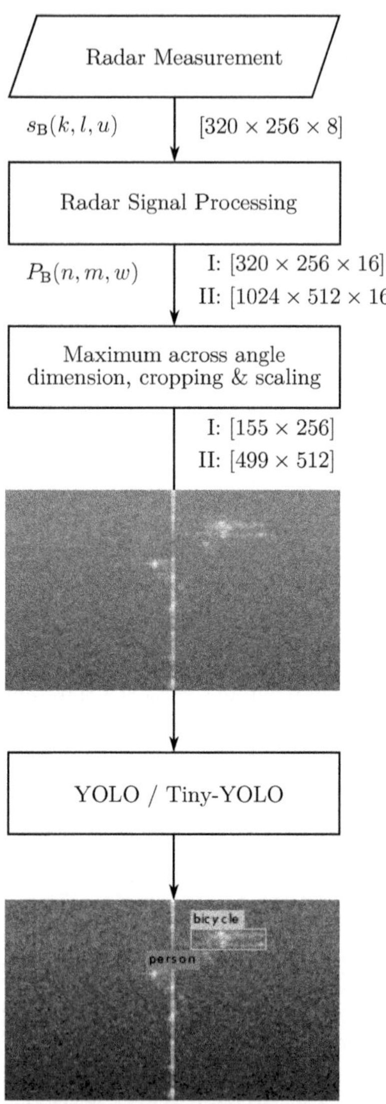

Figure 5.1: Overview of the radar-YOLO detection and classification system. Adapted from [PSRB19b].

5.1.3 You Only Look Once Object Detection

The YOLO system is a single-shot object detector first introduced in 2015 [RDGF15]. Since then, multiple iterations of the system have been released. For the radar detection system presented here, the third iteration—denoted YOLO v3 [RF18]—is used. The general concept of YOLO v3 object detection is based on dividing the input image into a grid of cells. A fixed set of predefined bounding box priors, the so called *anchors*, is then used at each of the grid cells to detect if an object of a certain class is present. A more detailed description of the system is introduced below.

a) **Network architecture.** The authors of the YOLO system [RF18] provide two differently sized networks: YOLO and tiny-YOLO. The first one uses a quiet deep network consisting of 53 convolutional layers—aptly named *darknet-53*—as a feature extractor. On the other hand, the tiny-YOLO network, as the name suggests, is a shallower network, meaning it has fewer layers. This results in faster detection time at the price of decreased accuracy. The detailed structure of a modified tiny-YOLO network (provided in [Boc19]) can be taken from Table 5.2. It is a fully convolutional neural network, i.e. no fully-connected layers are used. All convolution filters have either the size 3×3 or 1×1. Additionally to the convolution operations, pooling in form of max-pooling is applied throughout the network (the full sized YOLO network does not have these pooling layers). The "route" layers are shortcuts used to concatenate features at different stages of the network, while the detection happens at the "yolo" layers.

b) **Detection at three scales.** As can be seen from Table 5.2, there are three detection layers. The height and width of the feature maps directly before the "yolo" layers represent the size of the detection grid. For example, at the 16th layer the detection is performed with a 20×20 grid. Multi-scale detection showed to be beneficial for detecting smaller objects [RF18]. This is beneficial in urban automotive scenarios, since pedestrians are small targets in the range-Doppler-angle spectrum.

c) **Anchor boxes.** In order to detect the location and the dimensions of objects, YOLO uses a set of bounding box priors. Following [RF18], the anchor boxes that best fit the data and thus facilitate the training procedure are found by using k-means clustering on the bounding boxes present in the training data. A total of 9 anchors are found this way.

Nonetheless, not all anchor boxes are used for detection at every scale. Instead, they are assigned to the scale that best fits them, i.e. smaller anchors to higher resolutions and bigger anchors to lower resolutions. Figure 5.2 depicts the box priors assigned to the 20×20 resolution at one of the detections cells. In this example, it is evident, that the largest prior is already a good fit for the ground truth bounding box depicted in blue.

d) **Bounding box encoding.** At each scale, the network produces a 3-dimensional $C \times C \times [A \cdot (4 + 1 + 3)]$ tensor, where C is the number of rows and columns of the grid at the current scale and A the number of anchor boxes assigned to the scale. The

Table 5.2: Detailed structure of the tiny-yolo architecture

Layer	Type	Filters	Filter size/stride	Input size	Output size
0	convolutional	16	$3 \times 3 / 1$	$640 \times 640 \times 3$	$640 \times 640 \times 16$
1	max-pooling	-	$2 \times 2 / 2$	$640 \times 640 \times 16$	$320 \times 320 \times 16$
2	convolutional	32	$3 \times 3 / 1$	$320 \times 320 \times 16$	$320 \times 320 \times 32$
3	max-pooling	-	$2 \times 2 / 2$	$320 \times 320 \times 32$	$160 \times 160 \times 32$
4	convolutional	64	$3 \times 3 / 1$	$160 \times 160 \times 32$	$160 \times 160 \times 64$
5	max-pooling	-	$2 \times 2 / 2$	$160 \times 160 \times 64$	$80 \times 80 \times 64$
6	convolutional	128	$3 \times 3 / 1$	$80 \times 80 \times 64$	$80 \times 80 \times 128$
7	max-pooling	-	$2 \times 2 / 2$	$80 \times 80 \times 128$	$40 \times 40 \times 128$
8	convolutional	256	$3 \times 3 / 1$	$40 \times 40 \times 128$	$40 \times 40 \times 256$
9	max-pooling	-	$2 \times 2 / 2$	$40 \times 40 \times 256$	$20 \times 20 \times 256$
10	convolutional	512	$3 \times 3 / 1$	$20 \times 20 \times 256$	$20 \times 20 \times 512$
11	max-pooling	-	$2 \times 2 / 1$	$20 \times 20 \times 512$	$20 \times 20 \times 512$
12	convolutional	1024	$3 \times 3 / 1$	$20 \times 20 \times 512$	$20 \times 20 \times 1024$
13	convolutional	256	$1 \times 1 / 1$	$20 \times 20 \times 1024$	$20 \times 20 \times 256$
14	convolutional	512	$3 \times 3 / 1$	$20 \times 20 \times 256$	$20 \times 20 \times 512$
15	convolutional	40	$1 \times 1 / 1$	$20 \times 20 \times 512$	$20 \times 20 \times 40$
16	yolo	-	-	-	-
17	route [13]	-	-	-	-
18	convolutional	128	$1 \times 1 / 1$	$20 \times 20 \times 256$	$20 \times 20 \times 128$
19	upsample	-	-	-	-
20	route [19], [8]	-	-	-	-
21	convolutional	256	$3 \times 3 / 1$	$40 \times 40 \times 384$	$40 \times 40 \times 256$
22	convolutional	16	$1 \times 1 / 1$	$40 \times 40 \times 256$	$40 \times 40 \times 16$
23	yolo	-	-	-	-
24	route [21]	-	-	-	-
25	convolutional	128	$1 \times 1 / 1$	$40 \times 40 \times 256$	$40 \times 40 \times 128$
26	upsample	-	-	-	-
27	route [26], [6]	-	-	-	-
28	convolutional	128	$3 \times 3 / 1$	$80 \times 80 \times 256$	$80 \times 80 \times 128$
29	convolutional	16	$1 \times 1 / 1$	$80 \times 80 \times 128$	$80 \times 80 \times 16$
30	yolo	-	-	-	-

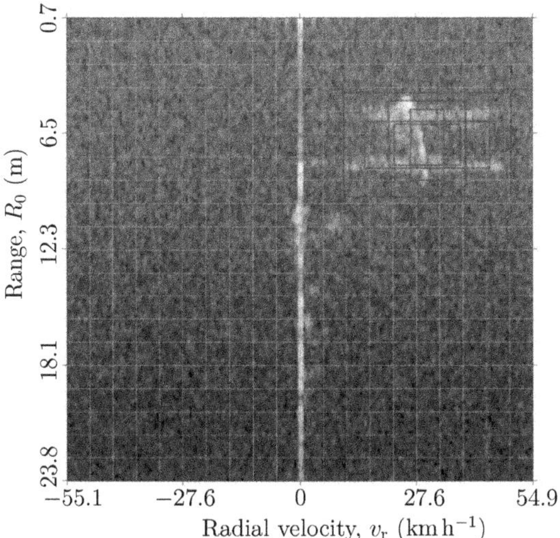

Figure 5.2: YOLO detection grid at the 20 × 20 resolution. The red rectangles depict the bounding box priors for a single grid cell. The ground truth bounding box is shown in blue. Adapted from [PSRB19b].

bounding box position and shape prediction is encoded in 4 values: the vertical and horizontal offsets from the center of the grid cell, and the width and height scaling factors from the priors. For each anchor at each grid cell one *objectness* score, which quantifies the confidence of the box actually containing an object, is given. Lastly, the class of the object task is encoded in the last 3 values, which represent the individual class probabilities (pedestrian, cyclist and car).

e) **Non-maximum suppression.** In order to avoid having more than one bounding box per detected object, the YOLO system employs a technique called non-maximum suppression (NMS). If two or more bounding boxes are very similar, only the box with the highest confidence score is kept and all other similar boxes are discarded. The similarity between two boxes is given by their intersection over union (IoU):

$$\mathrm{IoU}_{ij} = \frac{I_{\mathrm{ij}}}{U_{\mathrm{ij}}}, \tag{5.3}$$

where I_{ij} is the overlap area between boxes i and j and U_{ij} the area of their union.

5.1.4 Data Collection and Labeling

The dataset is gathered using the same test vehicle and setup as in Section 4.3. To train and evaluate this system, only stationary measurements, i.e. measurements where the ego-vehicle is not moving, are included. There are two main reasons for this. First, the data labeling task is more complex for this dataset than for the datasets used in Chapter 4, since bounding boxes need to be drawn tightly around the range-Doppler signature of the moving objects. By having the ego-vehicle stand still, the stationary objects are more easily ignored, which simplifies drawing the boxes around the moving targets. Second, in order to collect a higher number of pedestrian frames, it is helpful if the vehicle is parked in front of a street crossing or directly besides the sidewalk. When driving around the city, pedestrians are usually illuminated for shorter amounts of time, since they mainly walk on the sidewalk where no line of sight exists between them and the test vehicle.

The labeling process is aided by an automatic pre-labeling process using the lidar and camera sensors of the test vehicle. First, an object list is obtained from the lidar sensor and all objects found inside the radar FOV are saved. A picture taken with the front camera on the test vehicle is matched to the lidar measurement frame by means of their time-stamps. Thereafter, the position of the lidar objects is projected into the camera image and bounding boxes are drawn using the predicted objects dimensions provided by the lidar sensor. Using an already trained YOLO detection system provided by its authors [RF16], objects are detected on the camera image. The projected lidar objects overlapping the image objects detected by YOLO are subsequently matched to one another. A class is then assigned to the lidar objects by the camera objects with the highest IoU.

Following that, the classified lidar objects must be mapped into the radar RDA spectrum. This is done, analogously to Section 4.3.1, by means of a coordinate transformation. However, the lidar sensor only provides one velocity vector for the complete object and the goal here is to have a tight bounding box in range and Doppler dimensions. Therefore, in order to include the micro-Doppler signature of the different road users, the bounding box is enlarged in velocity dimensions by a certain amount. An OSCA-CFAR detection [KR13] is applied and the bounding box is fitted to the extent of the detections. Inevitably the windows will include false alarms, or not include the whole extent of the object, nonetheless this can be manually corrected later on.

After the pre-labeling process, the bounding boxes must be controlled and, if necessary, manually adjusted. This is done using the Image Labeler app from MATLAB [Mat20]. Figure 5.3 depicts the view during manually correction of the bounding boxes. The bounding boxes are shown over the OSCA-CFAR detections (with the angle dimension compressed analogously to Equation 5.1) and can be adjusted as needed. Changing the pre-selected class of the object is possible as well.

The number of bounding boxes per class of the resulting training and test datasets can be taken from Table 5.3. There are a total of four locations where measurements were performed. In order to decrease the correlation of training and test data, the training set contains frames from the first three locations and the test set from the fourth one. Additionally, 562 empty frames were added to the training data set with the aim to teach the network to recognize when a measurement only contains clutter and static objects. Including the empty frames, the training set amounts to a total of 4249 radar frames. The test set on the other hand does not contain empty frames and the total

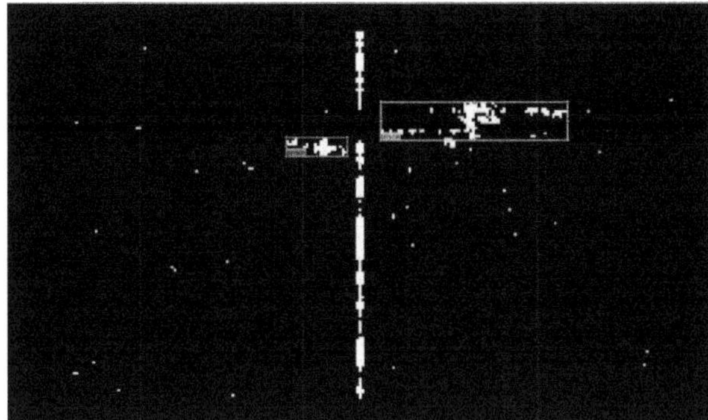

Figure 5.3: Data representation during the label correction process. The white squares indicate OSCA-CFAR detections. The user of the labeling GUI has to decide which detections belong to the object and which detections are false alarms or static objects.

Table 5.3: Distribution of the training and test datasets.

(a) Training set.

Class	Bounding boxes
Pedestrian	2445
Cyclist	1527
Car	785

(b) Test set.

Class	Bounding boxes
Pedestrian	204
Cyclist	533
Car	95

frame count amounts to 640. Because of the locations where the measurements were performed, both datasets contain subjects on a predominantly longitudinal trajectory in respect to the radar's boresight direction. Nonetheless, some laterally moving subjects are also included in the test set, as later shown in the evaluation part of the system (Section 5.1.6).

5.1.5 Training

The training process of a network as deep as *darknet-53* is a complex and highly time-consuming task, which also requires a very large dataset. Instead of training the network from the ground up, an often employed technique to overcome this is to start with a pre-trained network. This is known as transfer learning and has been used with success in a wide range of applications [TSK+18]. Specifically for the YOLO network, it has been shown that a network pre-trained for object detection on camera images can be successfully employed for other tasks, e.g. for breast masses in digital mammograms [AmAaP+18]. For this reason, a pre-trained network is used for the radar

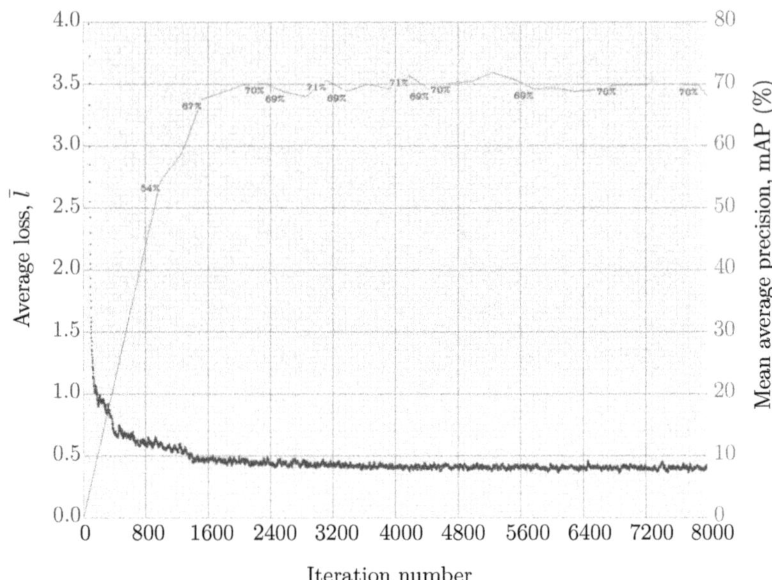

Figure 5.4: Training loss and evaluation mAP for the YOLO^{I} system.

object detection as well. For the full-sized network, as well as for the tiny network, weights, pre-trained on the Imagenet dataset [RDS+15] and made publicly available by the YOLO authors, are employed.

Training is done using two NVIDIA GPUs: a GeForce GTX 1080 Ti and a GeForce RTX 2080 Ti. The batch size to compute the loss and adjust the weights is set to 64 and the maximum number of training iterations to 8000. A starting learning rate of $\eta = 0.1$ is chosen and it is adjusted three times by scaling it by 0.1 after 1320, 3320 and 6640 training steps.

YOLO employs a custom loss function, which encompasses terms for the bounding box prediction—i.e. deviation from the anchors—, for the objectness scores and for the classification. In the case of the bounding box prediction a squared error function is used, while for both the objectness and the class predictions the binary cross-entropy is chosen [RF18].

Figure 5.4 depicts the training loss and the mAP computed with the evaluation set for the YOLO^{I} system. A rapid decline of the loss can be observed for the first 400 iterations, after which the decline starts slowing down. Another smaller drop in the loss is observed when the learning rate is adjusted at 1320 iterations. From there, it keeps decreasing very slowly until around 4000 iterations, from where it remains essentially constant. The mAP (computed on the test set) also stagnates early on and keeps oscillating between 69% and 70%.

Table 5.5: AP@0.5, mAP@0.5 and average detection time $\bar{t}_{\text{det}}$ for the different network configurations. Adapted from [PSRB19b].

	Tiny-YOLO^{I}	YOLO^{I}	Tiny-YOLO^{II}	YOLO^{II}
AP@0.5$_{\text{ped}}$ (%)	68.06	69.05	63.87	61.34
AP@0.5$_{\text{cyc}}$ (%)	65.16	70.33	65.55	60.69
AP@0.5$_{\text{car}}$ (%)	68.80	72.55	67.38	65.66
mAP@0.5 (%)	67.34	70.64	65.60	63.93
$\bar{t}_{\text{det}}$ (ms)	15.6	29.7	28.1	29.7

5.1.6 Evaluation

During the training procedure of each model, multiple checkpoints after a fixed number of iterations are saved. Then, the checkpoints that achieve the highest AP on the evaluation set are selected. The class specific AP, the mAP as well as the average detection time $\bar{t}_{\text{det}}$ of all 4 system configurations are laid out in Table 5.5. To compute this metrics, an IoU threshold of 0.5 is used, meaning that a detection is regarded as a true positive, if the predicted bounding box has the same class and an IoU of 0.5 or higher with the ground truth.

It is evident that the YOLO^{I} system with an mAP of 70.64% outperforms all other configurations. The average detection time for this system is $\bar{t}_{\text{det}} = 29.7\,\text{ms}$ making it, together with the YOLO^{II} system, the slowest configuration. It must be noted, that $\bar{t}_{\text{det}}$ only considers the inference time of the YOLO network and leaves out the whole radar signal processing chain, as well as any additional pre-processing steps.

The tiny-YOLO^{I} system configuration makes predictions twice as fast, while losing only around 3% mAP when compared to the YOLO^{I} system. On the other hand, increasing the number of FFT points does not bring any improvements, as shown by both systems using the configuration II. As a matter of fact, both systems where the signals get zero-padded before the FFTs have a lower mAP than their counterpart system without padding. A possible reason for this might be that the bigger size of the input images makes it more complex for the network to learn the relevant features. It must be noted, that the same training procedures and network architectures were used for configurations I and II. However, they were tuned specifically for the first configuration. Therefore, a change in the network structure or in the training regime could improve the results of the systems using configuration II.

Figure 5.5 depicts the precision vs. recall curves of the YOLO^{I} system for all three classes. As mentioned in Section 3.6, the shapes of these curves are summarized by their corresponding class specific AP. A certain operation point on the curve, e.g. one where the system's precision is favored at the cost of a lower recall, can be chosen by rising the detection threshold for the confidence score. YOLO's standard detection threshold is 0.25, which results in a precision of $p = 0.75$ and a recall of $r = 0.65$ for this system.

To finalize, multiple examples from the test set of detections with the YOLO^{I} system

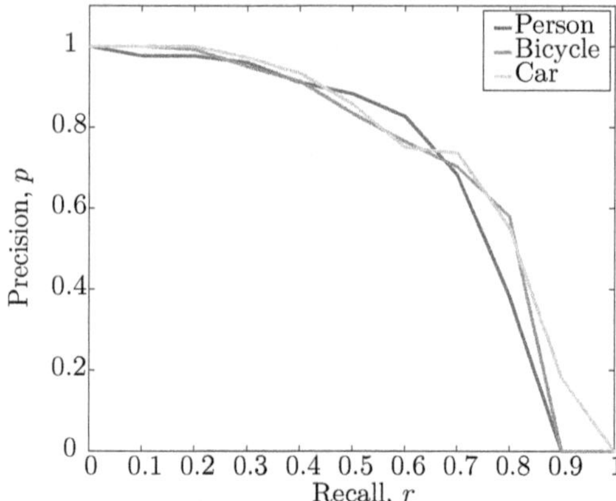

Figure 5.5: Precision vs. recall curves for the three different classes: persons, bicycles and cars. Adapted from [PSRB19b].

are analyzed. First, three scenarios where all moving objects within the radars FOV are successfully detected are shown in Figure 5.6. The predicted bounding boxes are displayed in a colored solid line bounding box with their respective class written on top. The ground truth box is delimited by a black dashed line with their fill color representing the ground-truth class. In Fig. 5.6a the scenarios shows the multi-class and multi-target capabilities of the system. Small targets, e.g. the pedestrian in Fig. 5.6a, medium-sized targets, e.g. the cyclist in Fig. 5.6a, as well as large targets, e.g. the car in Fig. 5.6b, are all detected by the system. Even difficult targets, such as the laterally moving pedestrian crossing the street depicted in Fig. 5.6c, are successfully detected and classified. The predicted bounding boxes are in all three scenarios close to the ground-truth.

The examples depicted in Fig. 5.7 show scenarios where the YOLO^{I} system fails to correctly detect or classify the moving objects in the radar's FOV. In Fig. 5.7a, a laterally moving cyclist is detected, but it is classified as a pedestrian. One possible reason for this is that its shape on the radar spectrum is similar to that of a longitudinally moving person. Figure 5.7c shows the same pedestrian as in Fig. 5.6c one frame later, but in this case, the pedestrian is not detected. The small azimuth angle and moving direction of the pedestrian result in quite a small footprint on the radar spectrum, as shown by the ground truth box. This makes it more difficult for the network to detect it. Figure 5.7b depicts a scenario where the ground truth bounding boxes of a pedestrian and a car are close together. The YOLO system detects them as a single large object of the car class. This behavior could be improved by adding multiple overlapping targets to the training set. However, overlapping scenarios are difficult to label on real measurements. A realistic simulation of such situations would therefore be very valuable. Alternatively, expanding the approach to include the angle extension of the objects would help with this problem, since they are clearly separated spatially a shown by the camera picture.

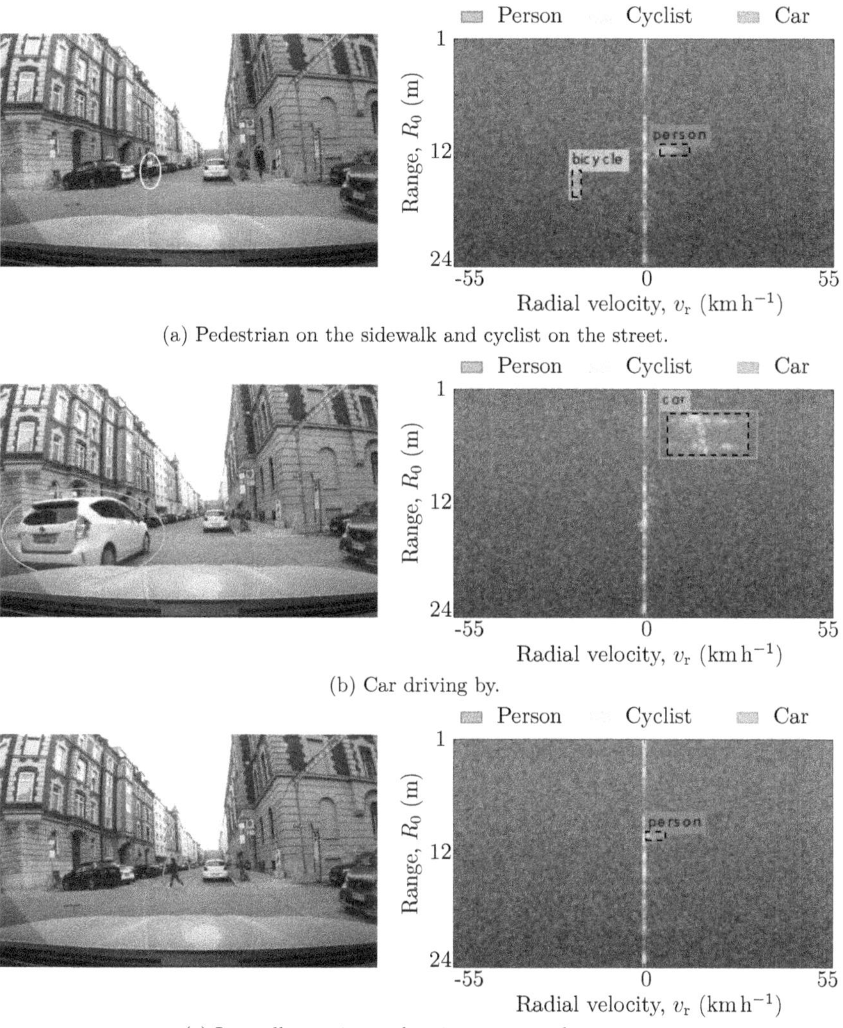

(a) Pedestrian on the sidewalk and cyclist on the street.

(b) Car driving by.

(c) Laterally moving pedestrian crossing the street.

Figure 5.6: Examples from the test data set of detections by the YOLO[I] system. YOLO detections are displayed by a box with a solid colored line and their class written on top. The ground truth box is marked with a dashed black line and the color of the shade represents the true class.

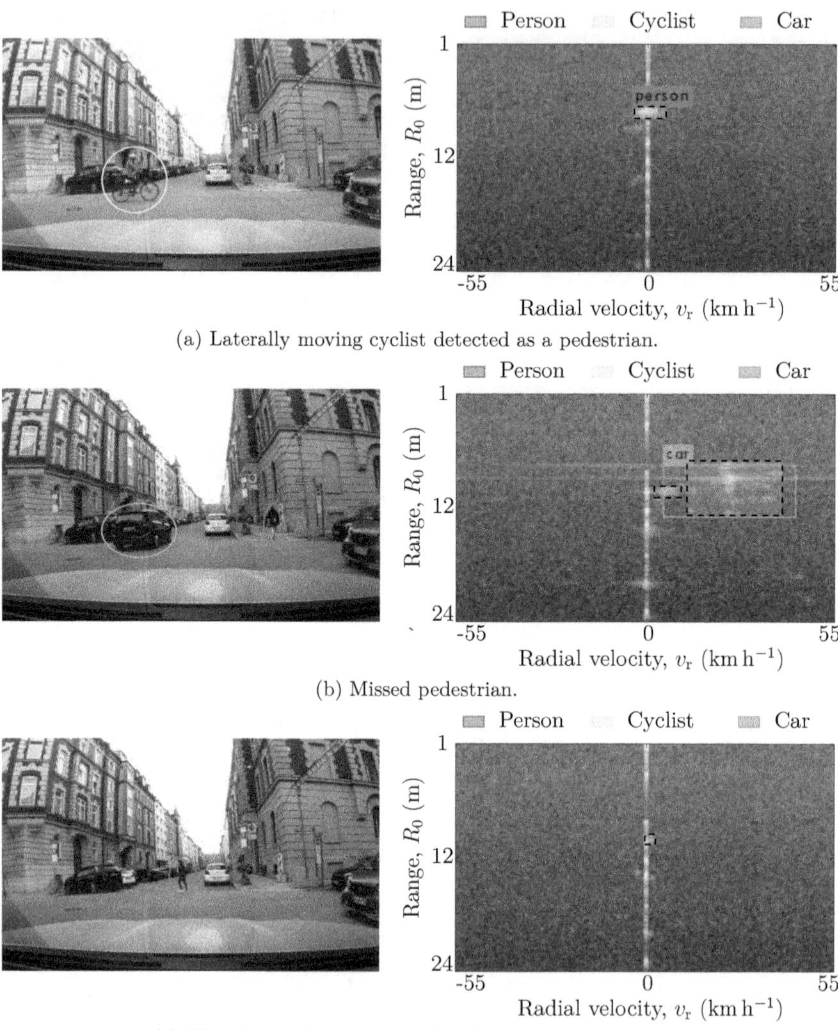

(a) Laterally moving cyclist detected as a pedestrian.

(b) Missed pedestrian.

(c) Missed laterally moving pedestrian crossing the street.

Figure 5.7: Examples from the test data set of misclassified and missed objects by the YOLO^{I} system. YOLO detections are displayed by a box with a solid colored line and their class written on top. The ground truth box is marked with a dashed black line and the color of the shade represents the true class.

5.2 Time Domain Detection

Up to this point, the employed algorithms are all based on treating different representations of the RDA spectrum (or cutouts thereof) as images. Nonetheless, the same information is contained in the time-domain signal as in its spectrum. For this reason, it should be possible to train a deep neural network directly on the time-domain signals. This section presents a novel approach—published in [PSRB21]—to detect targets and determine their range by running the raw intermediate frequency time-domain signal through a deep neural network, effectively replacing the usual FFT and CFAR detection procedures. The only closely related work found after a thorough search of relevant literature is a publication by Engelhardt, Pérez and Rao [EPR19], where a proof of concept of an occupancy grid created through a deep neural network fed with time-domain signals is presented. The concept of the system presented in the following section precedes [EPR19] and served as inspiration for it.

5.2.1 System Concept

The general concept of the neural network detection system is depicted in Fig. 5.8. Beginning with the radar measurement, since this system aims to perform detections on the range dimension only, a single chirp waveform is sufficient. The use of multiple receive channels would also be superfluous for the intended application. The single chirp waveform is configured the same ways as in all other systems presented in this work (see Table 2.1). Consequently, a radar measurement produces a one-dimensional array consisting of 320 samples.

The intermediate frequency signal $s_{\mathrm{B}}(k)$ is then high-pass filtered, in order to suppress the effects of transmitter leakage into the receiver path. After filtering, the time-domain signal is normalized to have zero mean and a standard deviation of 0.5:

$$x(k) = (s_{\mathrm{B}}(k) - \mu_{\mathrm{s}}) \cdot \frac{0.5}{\sigma_s}, \tag{5.4}$$

where μ_{s} and σ_{s} are the mean and standard deviation of the high-pass filtered signal. The normalized signal x is then run through the neural network, which in turn computes a probability that a target is present at each one of the discrete range bins. A threshold T is then applied to find the detections $z(n)$:

$$z(n) = \begin{cases} 1, & \hat{y}(n) > T \\ 0, & \hat{y}(n) \leq T \end{cases}. \tag{5.5}$$

5.2.2 Detection Network

State of the art object detection networks, such as YOLO, are not suitable for this kind of input data. This is due to the fact that the information is not spatially bound inside a region of the time domain signals, such as in the case of image object detection. For

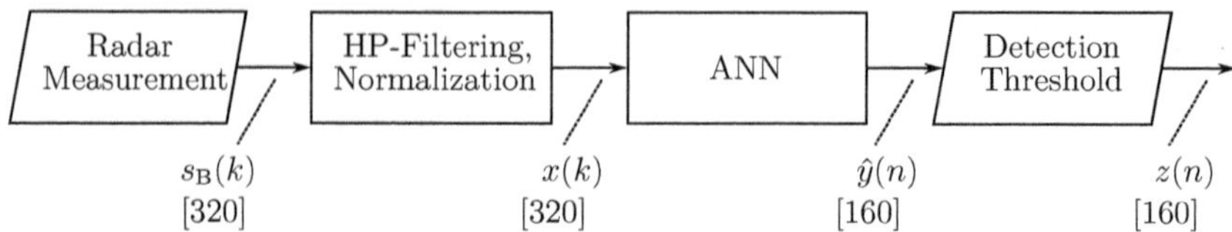

Figure 5.8: Overview of the time-domain detection system. Adapted from [PSRB21].

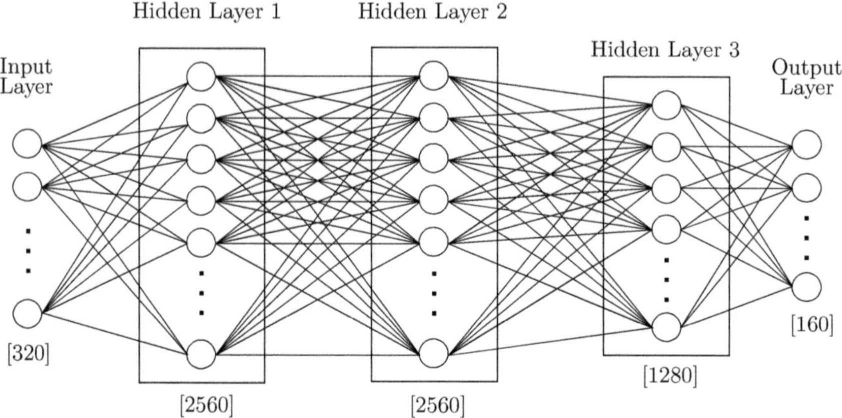

Figure 5.9: Proposed architecture of the artificial neural network for range detection. Source: [PSRB21].

the range detection task, the information is encoded within the frequency components of the baseband signal $s_B(k)$. Therefore, no bounding boxes enclosing this information can be drawn on the input data, as it is done for example in the frequency-domain detection.

Figure 5.9 depicts the architecture of the artificial neural network designed for this system. It is a multilayer perceptron consisting of one input layer, three hidden layers and one output layer. The number of neurons at each hidden layer are found empirically with help of the evaluation dataset. Preceding every hidden layer, the ReLU (Equation 3.27) is used as an activation function.

The range information is encoded in the output layer by assigning each neuron to a discrete range interval. This is done in analogy to the range spectrum obtained by computing the FFT of the time-domain signal. The range detection task is therefore reduced to solving a classification problem, where the input signal can belong to multiple classes (multi-label task), i.e. it may have multiple targets at different ranges. For this reason, the last activation is a logistic function (Equation 3.25) and not a softmax function (Equation 3.28), since the latter is better suited for single-label tasks.

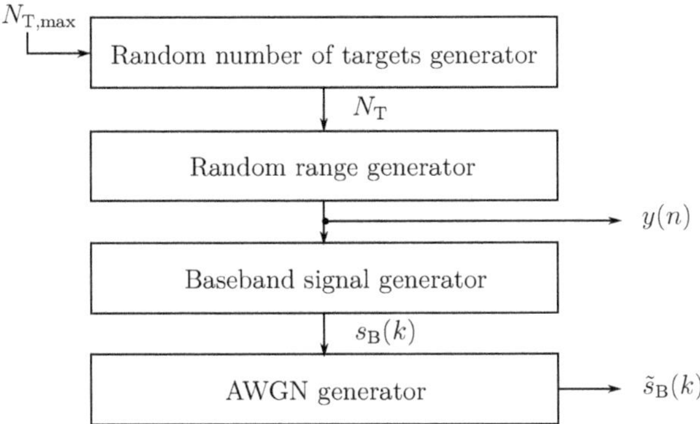

Figure 5.10: Random time-domain signals simulation. Source: [PSRB21].

5.2.3 Synthetic Data Generation

In order to create a large dataset with real radar measurements, the position of all reflective surfaces must be known. Additionally, a large variability in number of targets and their positions must be provided. This can not be achieved without a considerable time and cost effort. For this reason, it is decided to use synthetic data to train and evaluate the radar detection network. The baseband radar signal simulation process is shown in Fig. 5.10 and described in detail below:

1. **Number of targets generator.** As already mentioned, it is important that the network is able to detect multiple targets at different ranges simultaneously. To achieve this, signals are generated with a random number of targets. This block generates the number of targets N_{T} by drawing a number from a discrete uniform distribution $\mathcal{U}(0, N_{\mathrm{T,max}})$ between 0 and the pre-selected maximum number of targets $N_{\mathrm{T,max}}$.

2. **Random range generator.** The range of the targets is determined randomly as well. To do this, a range bin is selected by drawing a number from a discrete uniform distribution $\mathcal{U}(1, 160)$, where the upper boundary is equal to the dimension of the output vector. The bins corresponding to the drawn numbers are set to 1, while all remaining bins are set to 0. This simultaneously corresponds to the label $y(n)$ of the signal.

3. **Baseband signal generator.** This block's input are the ranges, where targets are located for the current frame. Using these ranges, it computes the baseband signal. However, they can only take on discrete values since they are drawn from the output range bins. This of course is not the case for real measurements. To better approximate real scenarios, a small range deviation δ_{R} is added to each range value R_0:

$$\tilde{R}_0 = R_0 + \delta_{\mathrm{R}}. \tag{5.6}$$

The range deviation δ_R is computed by:

$$\delta_\mathrm{R} = r \cdot \frac{\Delta R}{20}, \tag{5.7}$$

where r is a random number drawn from the discrete uniform distribution $\mathcal{U}(-9, 10)$ and ΔR the bin distance, which is equal to the radar's range resolution $\Delta R_0 = 15\,\mathrm{cm}$ in this system. This results in a discretization resolution of 7.5 mm for the simulated ranges.

Using Equation 2.22, the simulated baseband signal is computed by superimposing the real part of the contribution of all N_T targets:

$$\begin{aligned} s_\mathrm{B}(k) &= \sum_{i=1}^{N_\mathrm{T}} \mathrm{Re}\left(s_{\mathrm{B},i}(k)\right) \\ &= \sum_{i=1}^{N_\mathrm{T}} \cos\left(2\pi \cdot f_{\mathrm{B},i} \cdot \frac{k}{f_\mathrm{s}} + \phi_{0,i}\right), \end{aligned} \tag{5.8}$$

where $f_{\mathrm{B},i} = -\frac{B_\mathrm{sweep}}{T_\mathrm{up}}\frac{2}{c}\tilde{R}_{0,i}$ and $\phi_{0,i} = -f_\mathrm{c}\frac{2}{c}\tilde{R}_{0,i}$ stand for the beat frequency and phase term stemming from the i-th target. Only the real part of the signal is used, since the *radarbook*—which is later used to validate the system—also only samples one component of the signal.

4. **AWGN generator.** The last step is to add noise to the baseband signal. In this block, an additive white Gaussian noise (AWGN) channel is simulated. The final simulated baseband signal is then given by

$$\tilde{s}_\mathrm{B}(k) = s_\mathrm{B}(k) + \tilde{n}, \tag{5.9}$$

where the signal noise $\tilde{n}$ is drawn from a zero-mean Gaussian distribution $\mathcal{N}(0, \sigma_\mathrm{n})$ with standard deviation σ_n.

An example of a simulated signal is shown in Fig. 5.11. The time-domain signal (Fig. 5.11a) is composed in this case by the superposition of 9 reflections at multiple ranges. Figure 5.11b depicts the same signal in the frequency domain, i.e. the range spectrum. The corresponding ground truth (label) is overlaid on the range spectrum in red. Range bins with a target are marked with a "1" and range bins without a target with a "0".

It is worth noting, that all simulated targets have the same amplitude of "1", as seen in Equation 5.8. Adding amplitude variations, by either using the radar equation (Equation 2.6) or by assigning a random amplitude to the targets, complicates the learning procedure significantly and it is therefore decided to leave them out. In order to include them, different training regimes, with different loss functions and output representations, must be further investigated.

For the dataset, a total of 100,000 signals are simulated for the training and 10,000 for the validation dataset. The maximum number of targets allowed in one frame is set to $N_\mathrm{T,max} = 10$ and the noise variance is set relatively low to $\sigma_\mathrm{n}^2 = 0.0025$.

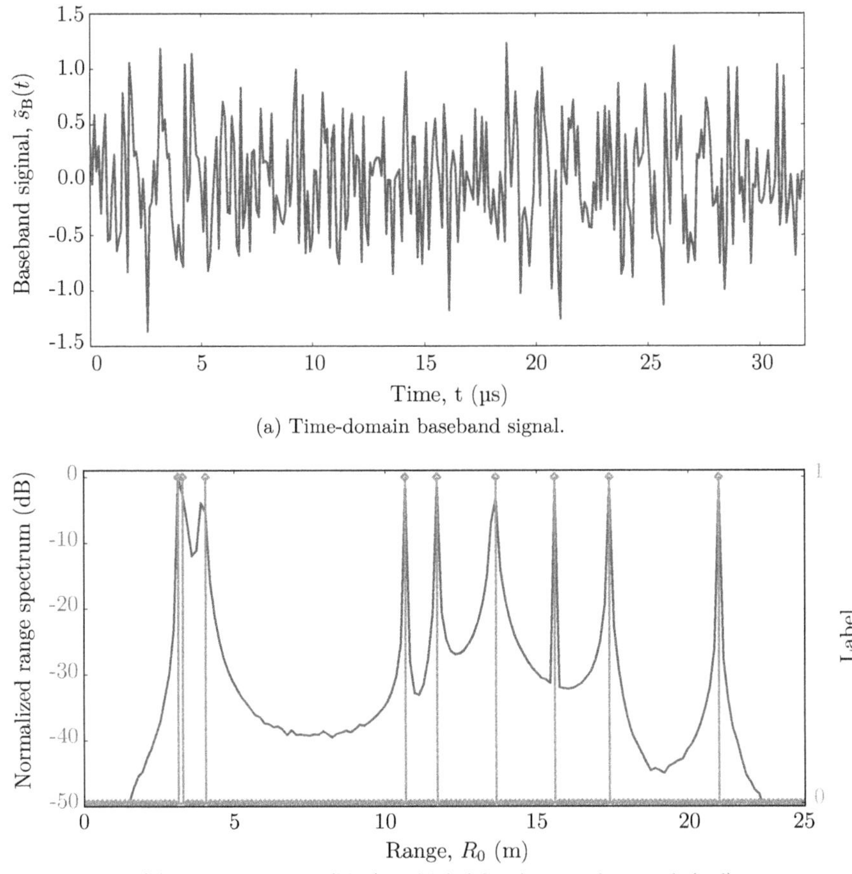

(a) Time-domain baseband signal.

(b) Range spectrum (blue) and label for the neural network (red)

Figure 5.11: Example of a simulated baseband signal with 9 targets in sight. The top plot (a) shows the time-domain signal, while the bottom one (b) shows the frequency-domain signal (range spectrum) as well as the corresponding label.

5.2.4 Training

The neural network is implemented using the TensorFlow software library [AAB+15]. Since the task at hand is effectively a classification problem, the cross-entropy loss (Equation 3.32) is selected. However, the dataset is quite imbalanced by design due to the fact that a maximum of 10 out of 160 range bins contain a target for every simulated frame. This complicates the learning procedure, since always predicting "no target" would already result in a small loss value. For this reason, a weighted cross-entropy loss function l_{wXE} is used in this case. It is defined as

$$l_{\mathrm{wXE}} = -(y \cdot \ln(\hat{y}) \cdot a + (1-y) \cdot \ln(1-\hat{y})), \tag{5.10}$$

where a is a positive weight. From Equation 5.10 can be seen, that a scales the weight of a positive error, i.e. a false negative. By choosing $a > 1$, the number of false negatives can therefore be reduced. On the other hand, choosing $a < 1$ increases this type of error.

The training procedure is carried out for a total of 1.2 million steps. Thereby, a batch consisting of 64 frames is used at each step to compute the training loss and subsequently update the weights. For the same reason, that a standard cross-entropy function is not appropriate to use as a loss function, the evaluation accuracy is not a good metric to monitor the training procedure. Therefore, the precision and recall metrics are employed.

Figure 5.12 depicts the precision and recall metrics during training for different values of a. These are computed using the evaluation dataset every 100 training iterations. It can be observed on Fig 5.12a that, by using the standard cross-entropy loss function ($a = 1$), a precision as high as $p \approx 98\%$ is possible. Nonetheless, a poor recall of only $r \approx 0.75$ can be achieved after 1.2 million training iterations, as seen in Fig. 5.12b.

As already mentioned, increasing the value of a results in a reduction of the number of false negatives and, thus, in an increase of the recall. For example, choosing $a = 10$ brings a significant improvement to the recall, bringing it to $r \approx 0.9$. Even though the precision is reduced by increasing a, it is not as significant as the improvement of the recall, since it still remains at $p \approx 0.95$. A good balance between increase in recall and fall in precision is found for $a = 20$. The chosen model ends up then with the validation metrics $r \approx 0.94$ and $p \approx 0.92$.

5.2.5 Evaluation With Simulated Targets

The performance of the neural network detector is evaluated with single and multi-target scenarios at different SNR levels. To do this, the simulation framework depicted in Fig. 5.10 is modified to produce a constant number of targets equal to either 1 or 5, depending on the scenario being considered. After producing the time-domain signals, their power is calculated and white Gaussian noise, whose variance is selected to achieve the desired SNR, is added.

The first scenario to be evaluated is the single-target scenario. In order to do this, 30 equidistant SNR levels, ranging from −20 dB to 9 dB, are considered. At each SNR level,

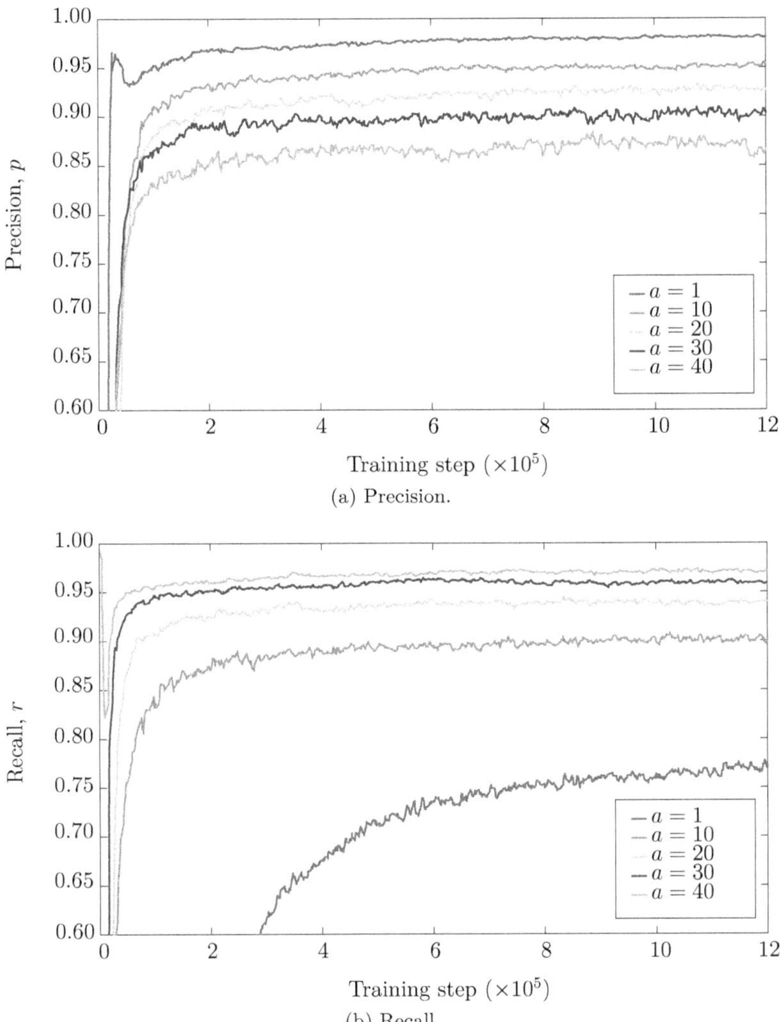

(a) Precision.

(b) Recall.

Figure 5.12: Precision and recall computed on the validation set for different values of the loss weight a.

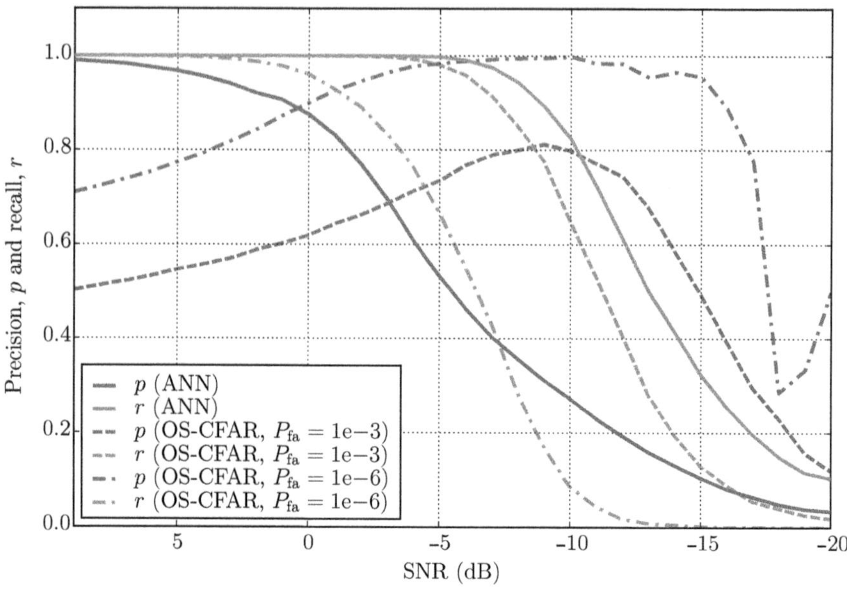

Figure 5.13: Precision and recall of the ANN detector and two different OS-CFAR detectors for 1 simulated target at different SNR levels.

10,000 signals—each one with a single target present at a randomly selected range—are simulated. The time-domain signals are then run through the neural network, producing the target probability vectors. A threshold of $T = 0.5$ is chosen to obtain the detections from the target probabilities.

Besides the ANN detector, two OS-CFAR detectors with different configurations are used as a baseline. The number of reference cells for these detectors is set to $N = 20$ and the rank for the noise level to $\kappa = 15$, which allows for up to 5 interfering targets inside the reference window. They differ however on the false alarm probability, with the first one set to have $P_{\text{fa}} = 1\text{e}{-3}$ and the second one $P_{\text{fa}} = 1\text{e}{-6}$. It should be noted, that the CFAR detectors work on an input signal with a considerably higher SNR than the ANN detector. For a given SNR of the time-domain signals, the CFAR detectors have approximately an additional 25 dB at the input, since the FFT brings a signal processing gain equal to the number of time-domain samples [Ric14, pp. 251].

Figure 5.13 shows the simulation results for the single target scenario. At high SNR levels, the recall of all 3 detectors is nearly perfect. The recall of the CFAR detector with the lower false alarm probability is the first one to degrade with decreasing SNR levels. This is due to the fact that the increased threshold necessary for a lower false alarm rate consequently results in a lower detection probability and, thus, in a lower

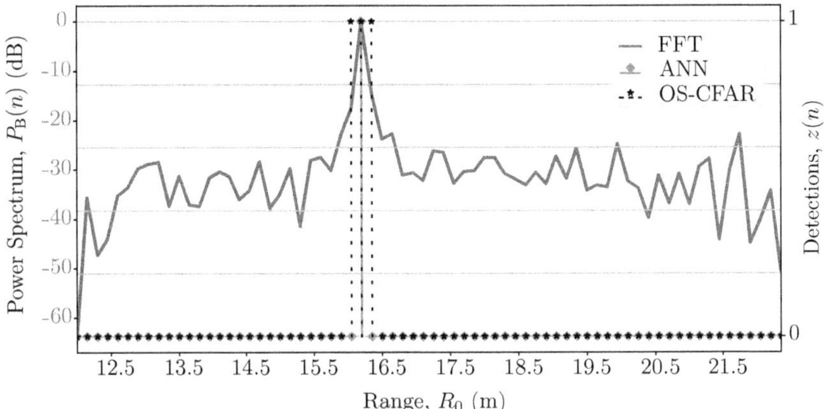

Figure 5.14: Example of detections by the ANN and OS-CFAR (P_{fa} = 1e−3) detectors at an SNR—prior to the FFT—of 10 dB. The ANN provides only one detection at the correct range bin, while the OS-CFAR detector provides two additional detections left and right of the correct range bin.

recall. The ANN detector provides a high recall up to an SNR of −10 dB, where it falls below $r = 0.9$.

The precision of the ANN detector deteriorates significantly sooner than the recall with decreasing SNR levels, which is expected given how the loss function is chosen to maximize the recall at cost of a worse precision. On the other hand, the CFAR detectors' precision is surprisingly low at high SNR levels. The reason for this is that when large targets are present, the CFAR detectors may detect more than one point for each peak in the range spectrum. Figure 5.14 depicts an example of this effect at an SNR of 10 dB. Since only one range bin is labeled as having a target, all other detections count as false positives, which lowers the precision. With decreasing SNR, this effect is naturally diminished, which in turn increases their precision. However, below a certain SNR, their precision starts sinking due to a decrease in the number of true positives.

The precision of the CFAR detector with $P_{fa} = 1e-6$ seems to increase again below an SNR of −18 dB. Nonetheless, this metric becomes unstable under those circumstances, due to the almost nonexistent number of true positives, which can be interpreted from the recall level of virtually zero. Therefore they are treated as outliers.

Figure 5.15 depicts the results of the simulation with 5 point targets (all with equal amplitude). Comparing this figure to Fig. 5.13, it can be seen that the metrics' curves are quite similar, meaning that the ANN system can also handle multi-target situations. Both its precision and recall stay above 0.9 up until an SNR of around −6 dB. However, at higher SNR values (above −6 dB), the CFAR detector with P_{fa} = 1e−3 has a better recall value. The increase in precision by all detectors can be explained by the higher

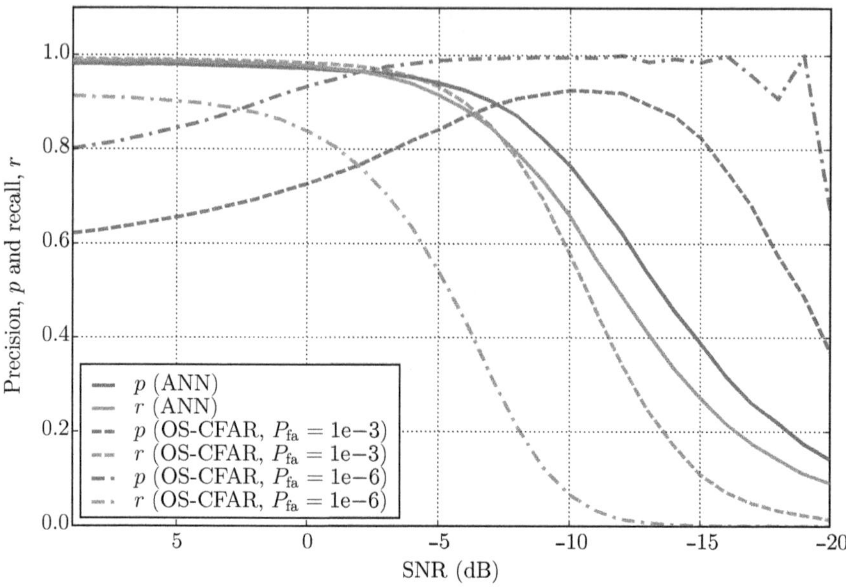

Figure 5.15: Precision and recall of the ANN detector and two different OS-CFAR detectors for 5 simulated targets at different SNR levels.

number of targets present and, thus, by the increase of true positives.

One drawback of this system is that it is trained with simulated reflections having all the same amplitude. The effects of amplitude variations on the performance of the ANN detector will be shown exemplarily with the same scenario used to plot the first data point in Fig 5.15, i.e. 5 targets at an SNR of 9 dB. However, a random scaling factor between 0.1 and 1 is added to the reflections. For this new conditions, the recall of the neural network drops from $r \approx 1$ to $r = 0.66$, since it misses a considerable amount of targets. On the other hand, the recall of the CFAR detector ($P_{\text{fa}} = 1\text{e}{-3}$) only drops to $r = 0.89$. For both detectors, the precision is not greatly affected. Figure 5.16 depicts a simulated frame with the aforementioned random amplitude variations. The CFAR detector detects all peaks (some with multiple detections) in the spectrum, while the ANN detector misses the target with the smallest amplitude. This shows, that the neural network can handle some variations in the amplitude, however they worsen its overall performance as shown by the drop in recall.

5.2.6 Evaluation with Real Measurements

Lastly, the system shall be evaluated with real radar measurements. In order to provide a meaningful quantitative evaluation, a large dataset with labeled positions is necessary.

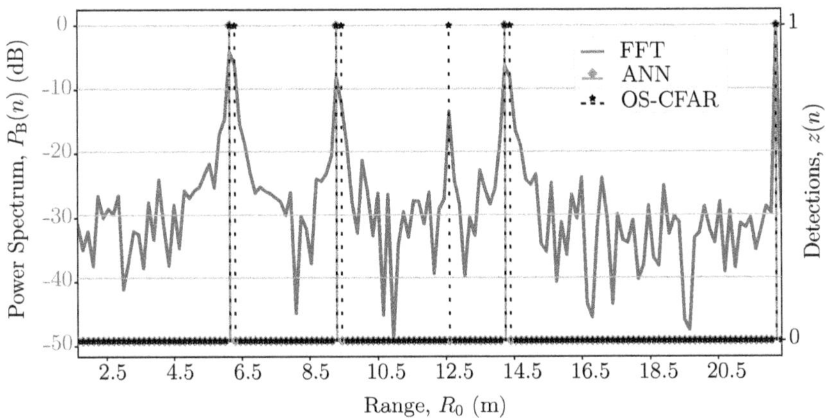

Figure 5.16: Detections by the ANN and OS-CFAR (P_{fa} = 1e−3) on a simulated frame containing 5 targets with randomly generated amplitudes. Adapted from [PSRB21].

Due to the lack of this, only a qualitative evaluation is performed and should therefore be regarded more as a proof of concept. The following measurements are performed in a room with absorbers, as shown in Fig. 5.17, in order to avoid reflections stemming from the walls and from other objects. The *radarbook* is used for the measurements with the same waveform parameters as in the simulation.

First, two corner reflectors separated by around 1.5 m from each other are contemplated. Figure 5.18 depicts the resulting range spectrum in blue and the neural network detections in red. Both corner reflectors are successfully detected at the correct ranges. While the reflector at a greater distance only causes one detection, the nearer reflector gives rise to two detections at consecutive range bins. Corner reflectors are however supposed to be ideal point targets. The reason for the dual detections can be traced back to the position of the corner reflector falling between two range bins.

A second measurement is performed with the corner reflectors close together at a distance of approximately 20 cm, which is close to the maximum achievable range resolution of 15 cm of the system. In this scenario, both corner reflectors can be detected by the ANN as well. The distance given by the ANN is nonetheless 30 cm, due to the discrete nature of the range measurements.

While these two measurements can not provide a quantitative evaluation of the system, they demonstrate the ability of the neural network to perform range detections on real radar measurements.

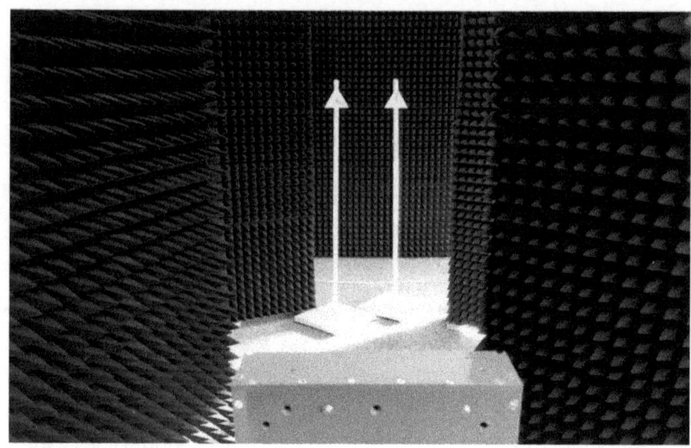

Figure 5.17: Measurement setup for evaluating the ANN detector. Two corner reflectors are placed in a room with absorbers. Source: [PSRB21].

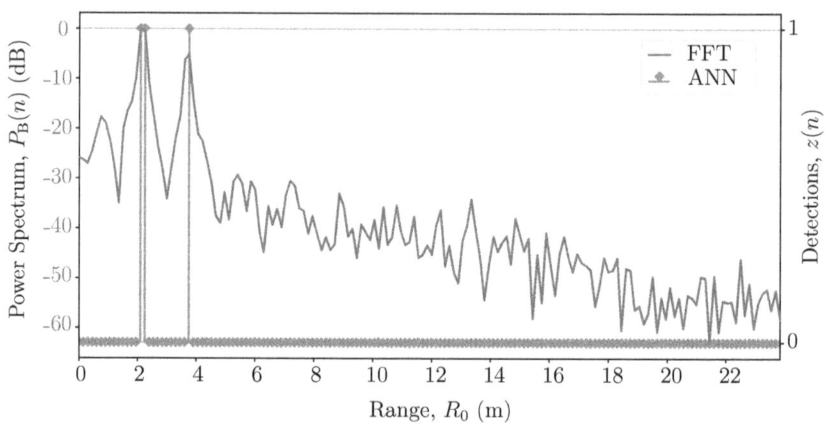

Figure 5.18: Measurement of two corner reflectors separated by 1.5 m. The range spectrum is shown in blue and the output of the ANN in red. Adapted from [PSRB21].

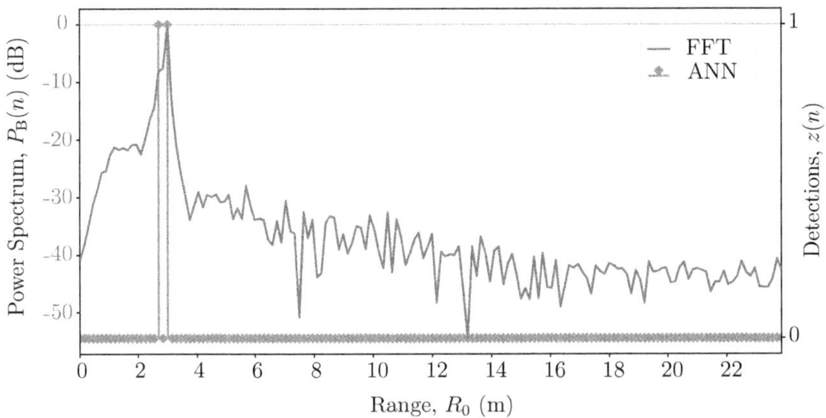

Figure 5.19: Measurement of two corner reflectors separated by 0.15 m. The range spectrum is shown in blue and the output of the ANN in red. Adapted from [PSRB21].

5.3 Concluding Remarks

The two systems in this chapter present deep learning approaches to perform detections based on the two lowest radar data layers (refer to Fig. 1.1). The first approach, based on layer L_1, uses a single-shot image detector, the so called YOLO system, to draw bounding boxes around subjects in range and Doppler dimensions, with the angle dimension compressed through a maximum function. Even with a relatively small dataset, the system achieves an mAP of around 70%. The main advantage provided by this approach is that multiple radar processing steps—i.e. detection, clustering, object creation and classification—are performed at once, avoiding the information loss caused by higher abstraction levels, all while potentially saving computing time.

The YOLO system is shown to be able to detect both small (pedestrians) and large (cars) objects on the radar spectrum, with lateral and longitudinal trajectories relative to the radar sensor. Nonetheless, there are still problematic situations, e.g. when the range-Doppler profiles of multiple objects overlap or are very close together. Two steps could be done in the future to improve this: (1) including overlapping bounding boxes in the trainings set and (2) expanding the YOLO framework to predict three-dimensional bounding boxes and, thus, include the angle information. The first measure is complicated, since labeling of range-Doppler profiles is not as straight forward as labeling, e.g., camera pictures. Especially when multiple objects overlap, it becomes difficult to assign the spectral components to the correct object. For this reason, it is also difficult to acquire a large scale dataset through outsourcing of the labeling procedure, since even for simple scenarios, an understanding of radar signals is needed. Therefore, developing realistic sensor models to simulate this scenarios would be extremely helpful, since no extra labeling procedure would be necessary. For the second measure, a radar sensor with a higher number of receive channels and consequently a better angle resolution is necessary. A MIMO radar system could be the solution in this case.

With the second system, the detection directly on raw, intermediate frequency time-domain signals (layer L_0) is explored. The approach consists in running the time-domain signal through an artificial neural network, which in turn predicts target probabilities at discrete range intervals. In order to train the network, a synthetic dataset consisting of multiple point-shaped targets at random ranges is generated. The system is evaluated with simulated signals at multiple SNR levels and compared with two OS-CFAR detectors. At high SNR levels, the ANN exhibits similar performance to the CFAR detectors and in some cases even better performance. At lower SNR levels, its recall remains higher than the CFAR detectors, at the cost of more false positives and, thus, lower precision. Finally, it is demonstrated that a system trained on simulated data can work with real radar measurements.

The main contribution of the second system is showing the possibility of applying a deep learning approach directly on raw radar data, effectively replacing not only the detection procedure, but also one of the fundamental radar signal processing steps, namely the Fourier transform. However, this is only the first step, since for automotive applications both angle and velocity measurements, as well as semantic information is required. Simply adding the missing dimensions to the input and output layers of this approach considerably increases the difficulty of minimizing the loss function, since the imbalance between positive and negative labels greatly grows. For this reason, different loss functions would need to be implemented.

Another big takeaway from this system is the ability to use a neural network, trained on synthetic data, on real radar data. Here, walking away from the point-shaped targets and towards realistic target models is also an important step for achieving a mature system.

6 Conclusion

This work presents multiple deep learning approaches for automotive radar signal processing. Thereby two main tasks are studied: radar target classification and radar target detection. For each of these tasks, two systems are developed and tested.

First, a radar system is selected to carry out the measurements throughout this work. The *radarbook* is chosen as the radar system because it operates at the desired frequency band of 77 GHz, it allows for free configuration of the waveform and it provides access to the baseband signal. An enclosure for the radar sensor, which includes a radome specially designed to minimize reflections, is also constructed. This allows to mount it on a test vehicle and perform test drives in the city.

The studies on radar-based classification begins with measurements of pedestrians, cyclists and cars. It is shown that these subjects show specific range-Doppler profiles, when contemplating the range-Doppler-angle power spectrum at a single angle bin. This is the case for longitudinal, as well as for laterally moving subjects. Even at small angles between the sensor and the subjects heading direction, where the radial velocity is near zero, some micro-Doppler components can be observed at close ranges, which is usually the case in urban scenarios. Based on this, the first approach is to treat the whole range-Doppler-angle power spectrum as an eight-channel image and classify it with a CNN. For this purpose, a dataset consisting of moving pedestrians, cyclists and cars is gathered by placing the radar sensor at the side of different streets. The system shows a remarkable performance, when tested with measurements gathered at the same location as those included in the training set. However, the performance is considerably lowered when tested with measurements from other street locations, which highlights the importance of gathering a large and heterogeneous dataset. Additionally, this approach does not allow for multiple targets to be present in the FOV within one measurement frame. The main contribution of this first system is demonstrating that single-shot radar based classification using deep learning is possible. Being able to perform a classification after one single measurement is a very important quality of a sensor system meant for autonomous vehicles, which must me capable of making split-second decisions.

The second classification approach has multi-target capabilities and is based on measurements from real urban scenarios. This system consists on using a CNN to classify fixed size ROIs, obtained trough a previous detection procedure, instead of whole datacubes. In this case, the *radarbook* is brought on a test vehicle to gather the dataset. Overall, this system exhibits a worse performance than the first one. This is expected, since the scenarios in this dataset are considerably more complex. Additionally, the input of this approach is 2-dimensional, leaving possibly helpful angle information out. Here, expanding the ROI to three dimensions and thus include the angle profile of targets would be beneficial to the classification performance. Furthermore, replacing the fixed-size ROI with one that fits tightly to the subjects would help mitigate the problem where multiple targets fall inside the same window. It is also shown that by applying a filter to aggregate classifications over time, the performance is improved. For future work, it makes sense to integrate this directly into the deep learning algorithm, e.g. with recurrent neural networks.

Furthermore, a mostly uncharted approach to radar target detection, i.e. leaving it to a deep learning network, is studied in this work. For this task two radar data layers are considered: the time-domain baseband signal (L_0) and its frequency spectrum (L_1). Starting with the latter, a system based on the real time object detector YOLO is presented. This approach consists on reducing the three-dimensional range-Doppler-angle power spectrum into a 2-dimensional image and then running it through the YOLO network, which in turn produces bounding boxes around the subjects together with a class prediction. The transition from 3D into 2D is achieved by applying a maximum function across the angle dimension. The main contribution of this novel system is that many of the classical radar signal processing steps—i.e. detection, clustering and classification—are performed by a single network, which circumvents the information loss at higher abstraction levels and can also potentially save computing time. It is shown that the system is able to handle large and small targets, such as pedestrians and cars. However, overlapping range-Doppler profiles are also problematic in this case. Here, working with simulated targets to learn these kind of scenarios or expanding the system into a three-dimensional detector would be helpful. Another important takeaway from this system is the possibility of using transfer learning, i.e. using a network pre-trained with images in this case, for radar object detection. This is helpful, since large radar datasets are currently not publicly available.

The second detection system explores the idea of using neural networks to perform detections directly on time-domain signals and thus replace the FFT and CFAR procedures. In order to create a large dataset, a synthetic point-target generator is developed. With this, 100,000 signals are generated for the training set and 10,000 for the evaluation set. As a baseline for evaluation, an OS-CFAR detector is chosen. Both detectors are then compared at different SNR values. The recall of the ANN is similar to the CFAR detector at high SNR values, however its precision is considerably better. At lower SNR values, the precision of the ANN quickly deteriorates, while the recall stays higher than the CFAR detectors. It is also demonstrated, that the system is able to detect targets on real radar measurements. From this system two things can be learned. First, it is possible to perform detections with a neural network directly on the first layer of the radar signal processing chain. Second, it is also feasible to train deep networks with simulated data, which later can be used on real data. This opens up the possibility for more complex detection schemes, e.g. the previously mentioned three-dimensional adaptation of the YOLO system, where labeling of real data is very complex.

6.1 Outlook

The systems presented in this thesis open up many opportunities for future work. First and foremost, as noted multiple times throughout this work, the datasets play a deciding role in the quality of the algorithms. For this reason, gathering a large-scale automotive dataset, which includes time-domain raw radar signals, should be a priority. The ideal dataset would include data from multiple sensors (camera, lidar, radar, etc.) and labels at different data layers. For example, in the case of radar sensor data, scenarios would ideally be labeled at the object layer—i.e. position and extension of objects in the vehicle's coordinate system—and at the radar spectrum layer—i.e. position and extension of objects in the range-Doppler-angle spectrum. For labeling at the object label, reference sensors and readily available tools can be used. More challenging, as shown in this work, is the labeling of the radar spectrum. This leads to the next point.

High quality simulations of radar measurements, which include micro-Doppler components, is an alternative worth further research and development. They would possibly eliminate not only the financial and time burden associated with test drives, but also the whole labeling process. Furthermore, they would be extremely helpful when studying the generalisability of deep learning approaches. Aspects such as sensor mounting position, number of transmit and receive channels and waveform parameters could all be investigated without the need of performing test drives every time.

In regards to deep learning algorithms for radar signal processing, object detectors which produce bounding boxes spanning the 3 dimensions of the radar spectrum should be researched. The issues caused by overlapping targets in range and velocity dimensions were shown by both the system with the YOLO object detector and the ROI classifier. Incorporating the angle dimension into the detection framework would help considerably with this. Since the range detector using time-domain signals showed promising results, end-to-end network architectures, which take the three-dimensional time-domain radar datacube as input and produce the previously mentioned three-dimensional bounding boxes as output, are an interesting research topic for future work. Additionally, fusing low level feature maps of radar, lidar and camera sensors is also an interesting field worth investigating.

Symbols

A_{R}	amplitude of the radar receive signal
a_{T}	time dependent amplitude of the radar transmit signal
$\bar{t}_{\mathrm{det}}$	average detection time
B_{sweep}	sweep bandwidth
c	speed of light
β	scaling factor in CFAR detection
D	antenna aperture diameter
z	detections
f_{B}	beat frequency
$f_{\mathrm{B,max}}$	maximum unambiguously measurable beat frequency
f_{c}	center frequency of a radar system
f_{CR}	chirp repetition frequency
f_{D}	Doppler frequency
$f_{\mathrm{D,max}}$	maximum unambiguously measurable Doppler frequency
f_{m}	frame rate
f_{s}	sampling frequency
f_{start}	start frequency of a frequency sweep
f_{stop}	stop frequency of a frequency sweep
f_{T}	transmit frequency of a radar system
f_{τ}	frequency difference due to time delay
f_{θ}	normalized spatial frequency
G_{R}	receive antenna gain
G_{T}	transmit antenna gain
θ_{3dB}	half power beamwidth
id	lidar object's ID
IoU	intersection over union
λ	wavelength
T	measurement track
a	accuracy in the context of machine learning
ϕ	activation function in the context of machine learning
α	neuron's activation in the context of machine learning
AP	average precision in the context of machine learning
b	bias variable in the context of machine learning

J	training error in the context of machine learning
fn	false negatives
fp	false positives
x	input values in the context of machine learning
η	learning rate in the context of machine learning, scaling constant in the context of discrete Bayes filtering
l	loss in the context of machine learning
mAP	mean average precision in the context of machine learning
n_{h}	number of neurons in a hidden layer of an MLP
n_{x}	number of units at the input layer of an MLP
n_{y}	number of units at the output layer of an MLP
y	true values in the context of machine learning
$\hat{y}$	output values in the context of machine learning
p	precision in the context of machine learning
r	recall in the context of machine learning
tn	true negatives
tp	true positives
w	weight variables in the context of machine learning
L	number of chirps in a frame
U	number of antennas in a ULA
K	number of samples in a chirp
O	lidar object
Ω	lidar sensor's object list
κ	OS CFAR rank
P_{B}	power spectrum of the baseband signal
P_{R}	receive radar power
P_{T}	transmit radar power
P_{fa}	false alarm probability
ϕ_0	arbitrary constant phase term of a radar signal
ϕ_{T}	phase of the transmit signal
R_0	range from radar system
R_{Fra}	Fraunhofer distance
$R_{0,\mathrm{max}}$	maximum unambiguously measurable range
x_c	sates of the random variable X
X	random state variable
σ_{r}	radar cross section
d	distance between neighboring antennas in a ULA
S_{B}	frequency domain radar baseband signal
s_{B}	time domain radar baseband signal
$s_{\mathrm{B}}^{\mathrm{I}}$	in phase component of radar baseband signal
$s_{\mathrm{B}}^{\mathrm{Q}}$	quadrature component of the radar baseband signal
s_{R}	radar receive signal

s_T	radar transmit signal
β_x	spatial bandwidth
F_x	spatial frequency
t	time
T_CR	chirp repetition interval
T_m	radar frame measurement duration
T_up	ramp up time
τ	round trip time of flight in the context of radar signal processing, discrete time index in the context of the joint lidar and radar classification system
θ	azimuth angle
T	detection threshold
T	detection threshold
ts	lidar object's time stamp
Ψ	radar measurement tupel
$v_\mathrm{r,max}$	maximum unambiguously measurable radial velocity
v_r	relative radial velocity

Acronyms

ABS	anti-lock braking system
ACC	adaptive cruise control
ADAS	advanced driver-assistance systems
ADC	analog-to-digital converter
ADS	automated driving system
AEB	autonomous emergency braking
AFE	analog front end
ANN	artificial neural network
AOA	angle of arrival
AWGN	additive white Gaussian noise
CA	cell averaging
CFAR	constant false alarm rate
CNN	convolutional neural network
CUT	cell under test
CW	continuous wave
DBF	discrete Bayes filter
DFT	discrete Fourier transform
EIRP	equivalent isotropic radiated power
FFT	fast Fourier transform
FMCW	frequency modulated continuous wave
FOV	field of view
ISM	industry, scientific and medical
KNN	k-nearest neighbors
LDWS	lane departure warning system
LFMCW	linear frequency modulated continuous wave
LNA	low noise amplifier
LPF	low-pass filter
LSTM	long short-term memory
MIMO	multiple-input multiple-output
MLP	multi-layer perceptron
NMS	non-maximum suppression
OS	order statistics
RCS	radar cross section

RDA	range-Doppler-angle
ReLU	rectified linear unit
ROI	region of interest
ROS	robot operating system
SGD	stochastic gradient descent
SNR	signal-to-noise ratio
STFT	short time fast Fourier transform
SVM	support vector machine
ULA	uniform linear array
UWB	ultra wide band
VCO	voltage controlled oscillator
VRU	vulnerable road user
YOLO	You Only Look Once

Bibliography

[AAB+15] Martín Abadi, Ashish Agarwal, Paul Barham, Eugene Brevdo, Zhifeng Chen, Craig Citro, Greg S. Corrado, Andy Davis, Jeffrey Dean, Matthieu Devin, Sanjay Ghemawat, Ian Goodfellow, Andrew Harp, Geoffrey Irving, Michael Isard, Yangqing Jia, Rafal Jozefowicz, Lukasz Kaiser, Manjunath Kudlur, Josh Levenberg, Dandelion Mané, Rajat Monga, Sherry Moore, Derek Murray, Chris Olah, Mike Schuster, Jonathon Shlens, Benoit Steiner, Ilya Sutskever, Kunal Talwar, Paul Tucker, Vincent Vanhoucke, Vijay Vasudevan, Fernanda Viégas, Oriol Vinyals, Pete Warden, Martin Wattenberg, Martin Wicke, Yuan Yu, and Xiaoqiang Zheng. TensorFlow: Large-scale machine learning on heterogeneous systems, 2015. Software available from tensorflow.org, [Accessed]: 04.06.2020.

[AmAaP+18] Mohammed A. Al-masni, Mugahed A. Al-antari, Jeong-Min Park, Geon Gi, Tae-Yeon Kim, Patricio Rivera, Edwin Valarezo, Mun-Taek Choi, Seung-Moo Han, and Tae-Seong Kim. Simultaneous detection and classification of breast masses in digital mammograms via a deep learning YOLO-based CAD system. *Computer Methods and Programs in Biomedicine*, 157:85 – 94, 2018.

[BB06] M. Buhren and Bin Yang. Simulation of automotive radar target lists using a novel approach of object representation. In *2006 IEEE Intelligent Vehicles Symposium*, pages 314–319, June 2006.

[Ben86] Benz & Co. Fahrzeug mit Gasmotorenbetrieb, Patent DRP 37435, January 1886.

[BFR12] A. Bartsch, F. Fitzek, and R. H. Rasshofer. Pedestrian recognition using automotive radar sensors. *Advances in Radio Science*, 10:45–55, 2012.

[BML+18] P. Berthold, M. Michaelis, T. Luettel, D. Meissner, and H. Wuensche. An abstracted radar measurement model for extended object tracking. In *2018 21st International Conference on Intelligent Transportation Systems (ITSC)*, pages 3866–3872, Nov 2018.

[Boc19] Alexey Bochkovskiy. darknet, 2019. GitHub repository [Online]. Available: `https://github.com/AlexeyAB/darknet` [Accessed]: 25.05.2020.

[BSMM08] Ilja N. Bronstein, Konstantin A. Semendjajew, Gerhard Musiol, and Heiner Mühlig. *Taschenbuch der Mathematik*. Wissenschaftlicher Verlag Harri Deutsch GmbH, 7th edition edition, 2008.

[BTT90] Ronan Boulic, Nadia Magnenat Thalmann, and Daniel Thalmann. A global human walking model with real-time kinematic personification. *The visual computer*, 6(6):344–358, 1990.

[Cad90] J. A. Cadzow. Multiple source location-the signal subspace approach. *IEEE Transactions on Acoustics, Speech, and Signal Processing*, 38(7):1110–1125, July 1990.

[Che00] V. C. Chen. Analysis of radar micro-doppler with time-frequency transform. In *Proceedings of the Tenth IEEE Workshop on Statistical Signal and Array Processing (Cat. No.00TH8496)*, pages 463–466, Aug 2000.

[Chr04] Christian Hülsmeyer. Verfahren, um entfernte metallische Gegenstände mittels elektrischer Wellen einem Beobachter zu melden., Patent DRP 37435, April 1904.

[CLHW06] V. C. Chen, F. Li, S. . Ho, and H. Wechsler. Micro-doppler effect in radar: phenomenon, model, and simulation study. *IEEE Transactions on Aerospace and Electronic Systems*, 42(1):2–21, Jan 2006.

[CT65] James W. Cooley and John W. Tukey. An algorithm for the machine calculation of complex fourier series. *Mathematics of Computation*, 19(90):297–301, 1965.

[DHS01] Richard O Duda, Peter E Hart, and David G Stork. *Pattern classification*. John Wiley & Sons, Inc., 2nd edition edition, 2001.

[DLS+19] Jürgen Dickmann, Jakob Lombacher, Ole Schumann, Nicolas Scheiner, Saeid K Dehkordi, Tilmann Giese, and Bharanidhar Duraisamy. Radar for autonomous driving–paradigm shift from mere detection to semantic environment understanding. In *Fahrerassistenzsysteme 2018*, pages 1–17. Springer, 2019.

[EKS+96] Martin Ester, Hans-Peter Kriegel, Jörg Sander, Xiaowei Xu, et al. A density-based algorithm for discovering clusters in large spatial databases with noise. In *Kdd*, volume 96, pages 226–231, 1996.

[EPBB20] Thomas Eder, Alexander Prinz, Ludwig Brabetz, and Erwin Biebl. *Szenarienbasierte Validierung eines hybriden Radarmodells für Test und Absicherung automatisierter Fahrfunktionen*, pages 21–43. Springer Berlin Heidelberg, Berlin, Heidelberg, 2020.

[EPR19] N. Engelhardt, R. Pérez, and Q. Rao. Occupancy Grids Generation Using Deep Radar Network for Autonomous Driving. In *2019 IEEE Intelligent Transportation Systems Conference (ITSC)*, pages 2866–2871, Oct 2019.

[ETS16] ETSI EN 301 091-1. Short Range Devices; Transport and Traffic Telematics (TTT); Radar equipment operating in the 76 GHz to 77 GHz range; Harmonised Standard covering the essential requirements of article 3.2 of Directive 2014/53/EU; Part 1: Ground based vehicular radar. Standard, European Telecommunications Standards Institute (ETSI), November 2016. [Online]. Available: `https://www.etsi.org/deliver/etsi_en/301000_301099/30109101/02.01.01_30/en_30109101v020101v.pdf` [Accessed]: 03.04.2020.

[ETS17a] ETSI EN 302 264. Short Range Devices; Transport and Traffic Telematics (TTT); Short Range Radar equipment operating in the 77 GHz to 81 GHz band; Harmonised Standard covering the essential requirements of article 3.2 of Directive 2014/53/EU. Standard, European Telecommunications Standards Institute (ETSI), February 2017. [Online]. Available: `https://www.etsi.org/deliver/etsi_en/302200_302299/302264/02.01.01_30/en_302264v020101v.pdf` [Accessed]: 03.04.2020.

[ETS17b] ETSI EN 302 288. Ultra-wideband radar equipment operating in the 24,25 GHz to 26,65 GHz range. Standard, European Telecommunications Standards Institute (ETSI), May 2017. [Online]. Available: `https://www.etsi.org/deliver/etsi_en/302200_302299/302288/02.01.01_60/en_302288v020101p.pdf` [Accessed]: 03.04.2020.

[Eur18a] European Commission. Traffic safety basic facts on cyclists, June 2018. [Online]. Available: `https://ec.europa.eu/transport/road_safety/sites/roadsafety/files/pdf/statistics/dacota/bfs20xx_cyclists.pdf` [Accessed]: 24.07.2020.

[Eur18b] European Commission. Traffic safety basic facts on pedestrians, June 2018. [Online]. Available: `https://ec.europa.eu/transport/road_safety/sites/roadsafety/files/pdf/statistics/dacota/bfs20xx_pedestrians.pdf` [Accessed]: 24.07.2020.

[EVGW+10] Mark Everingham, Luc Van Gool, Christopher KI Williams, John Winn, and Andrew Zisserman. The pascal visual object classes (voc) challenge. *International journal of computer vision*, 88(2):303–338, 2010.

[Fri98] Gerhard Friedsam. *Bestimmung der komplexen Permittivität und Permeabilität im Millimeterwellenbereich.* PhD thesis, Technische Universität München, 1998.

[FRR06] Florian Fölster, Hermann Rohling, and Henning Ritter. Observation of a walking pedestrian with a 24ghz automotive radar sensor. In *German Microwave Conf., Karlsruhe, Germany*, 2006.

[Gal16] Gaspare Galati. *Scops Owls and Bats—Recent Radar Developments*, pages 265–301. Springer International Publishing, Cham, 2016.

[GBB11] Xavier Glorot, Antoine Bordes, and Yoshua Bengio. Deep sparse rectifier neural networks. In *Proceedings of the Fourteenth International Conference on Artificial Intelligence and Statistics*, volume 15 of *Proceedings of Machine Learning Research*, pages 315–323, Fort Lauderdale, FL, USA, 11–13 Apr 2011.

[HR12] S. Heuel and H. Rohling. Pedestrian classification in automotive radar systems. In *2012 13th International Radar Symposium*, pages 39–44, May 2012.

[HTS+12] J. Hasch, E. Topak, R. Schnabel, T. Zwick, R. Weigel, and C. Waldschmidt. Millimeter-wave technology for automotive radar sensors in the 77 ghz frequency band. *IEEE Transactions on Microwave Theory and Techniques*, 60(3):845–860, 2012.

[HW62] David H Hubel and Torsten N Wiesel. Receptive fields, binocular interaction and functional architecture in the cat's visual cortex. *The Journal of physiology*, 160(1):106–154, 1962.

[Inr15a] Inras GmbH. *AN77-08 Correcting the Effects of Sequential Sampling*, 2015.

[Inr15b] Inras GmbH. *MIMO-77-TX4RX8 Frontend (User Manual)*, 2015. [Online]. Available: `http://www.inras.at/uploads/media/MIMO-77-TX4RX8.pdf` [Accessed]: 08.04.2020.

[J3018] SAE J3016. Taxonomy and definitions for terms related to driving automation systems for on-road motor vehicles. Standard, SAE International, June 2018.

[JAA16] B. Jokanovic, M. Amin, and F. Ahmad. Radar fall motion detection using deep learning. In *2016 IEEE Radar Conference (RadarConf)*, pages 1–6, 2016.

[KB14] Diederik P. Kingma and Jimmy Ba. Adam: A method for stochastic optimization, 2014.

[KBK+15] D. Kellner, M. Barjenbruch, J. Klappstein, J. Dickmann, and K. Dietmayer. Wheel extraction based on micro doppler distribution using high-resolution radar. In *2015 IEEE MTT-S International Conference on Microwaves for Intelligent Mobility (ICMIM)*, pages 1–4, April 2015.

[KCK+20] Woosuk Kim, Hyunwoong Cho, Jongseok Kim, Byungkwan Kim, and Seongwook Lee. Yolo-based simultaneous target detection and classification in automotive fmcw radar systems. *Sensors*, 20(10):2897, 2020.

[KM16] Y. Kim and T. Moon. Human detection and activity classification based on micro-doppler signatures using deep convolutional neural networks. *IEEE Geoscience and Remote Sensing Letters*, 13(1):8–12, 2016.

[KPDA60] J. R. Klauder, A. C. Price, S. Darlington, and W. J. Albersheim. The theory and design of chirp radars. *The Bell System Technical Journal*, 39(4):745–808, July 1960.

[KR13] M. Kronauge and H. Rohling. Fast two-dimensional cfar procedure. *IEEE Transactions on Aerospace and Electronic Systems*, 49(3):1817–1823, 2013.

[KR14] M. Kronauge and H. Rohling. New chirp sequence radar waveform. *IEEE Transactions on Aerospace and Electronic Systems*, 50(4):2870–2877, October 2014.

[Kra20] Kraftfahrt-Bundesamt. Bestand in den Jahren 1960 bis 2020 nach Fahrzeugklassen, 2020. [Online]. Available: `https://www.kba.de/DE/Statistik/Fahrzeuge/Bestand/FahrzeugklassenAufbauarten/fz_b_fzkl_aufb_archiv/2020/b_fzkl_zeitreihe.html` [Accessed]: 20.07.2020.

[Kro14] Matthias Kronauge. *Waveform Design for Continuous Wave Radars*. Cuvillier Verlag Göttingen, 2014.

[KSH12] Alex Krizhevsky, Ilya Sutskever, and Geoffrey E Hinton. Imagenet classification with deep convolutional neural networks. In *Advances in neural information processing systems*, pages 1097–1105, 2012.

[KV96] H. Krim and M. Viberg. Two decades of array signal processing research: the parametric approach. *IEEE Signal Processing Magazine*, 13(4):67–94, July 1996.

[LGK+16] Jaime Lien, Nicholas Gillian, M. Emre Karagozler, Patrick Amihood, Carsten Schwesig, Erik Olson, Hakim Raja, and Ivan Poupyrev. Soli: Ubiquitous gesture sensing with millimeter wave radar. *ACM Trans. Graph.*, 35(4), July 2016.

[LHDW15] J. Lombacher, M. Hahn, J. Dickmann, and C. Wöhler. Detection of arbitrarily rotated parked cars based on radar sensors. In *2015 16th International Radar Symposium (IRS)*, pages 180–185, 2015.

[LHDW17] J. Lombacher, M. Hahn, J. Dickmann, and C. Wöhler. Object classification in radar using ensemble methods. In *2017 IEEE MTT-S International Conference on Microwaves for Intelligent Mobility (ICMIM)*, pages 87–90, 2017.

[LSMD05] D. T. Linzmeier, M. Skutek, M. Mekhaiel, and K. C. J. Dietmayer. A pedestrian detection system based on thermopile and radar sensor data fusion. In *2005 7th International Conference on Information Fusion*, volume 2, pages 8 pp.–, 2005.

[Lyo10] R.G. Lyons. *Understanding Digital Signal Processing*. Pearson Education, 3rd edition edition, 2010.

[Mat20] MathWorks. Getting started with the image labeler, 2020. [Online]. Available: `https://de.mathworks.com/help/vision/ug/get-started-with-the-image-labeler.html` [Accessed]: 05.06.2020.

[MB01] S. Milch and M. Behrens. Pedestrian detection with radar and computer vision, 2001.

[MEA+14] P. Molchanov, K. Egiazarian, J. Astola, A. Totsky, S. Leshchenko, and M. P. Jarabo-Amores. Classification of aircraft using micro-doppler bicoherence-based features. *IEEE Transactions on Aerospace and Electronic Systems*, 50(2):1455–1467, April 2014.

[MFA+19] B. Major, D. Fontijne, A. Ansari, R. T. Sukhavasi, R. Gowaikar, M. Hamilton, S. Lee, S. Grzechnik, and S. Subramanian. Vehicle detection with automotive radar using deep learning on range-azimuth-doppler tensors. In *2019 IEEE/CVF International Conference on Computer Vision Workshop (ICCVW)*, pages 924–932, 2019.

[MHdW+14] Pavlo Molchanov, Ronny I.A. Harmanny, Jaco J.M. de Wit, Karen Egiazarian, and Jaakko Astola. Classification of small uavs and birds by micro-doppler signatures. *International Journal of Microwave and Wireless Technologies*, 6(3-4):435–444, 2014.

[MP43] Warren S McCulloch and Walter Pitts. A logical calculus of the ideas immanent in nervous activity. *The bulletin of mathematical biophysics*, 5(4):115–133, 1943.

[MP88] Marvin Minsky and Seymour A Papert. *Perceptrons: An introduction to computational geometry*. MIT press, 1988.

[Mur12] Kevin P. Murphy. *Machine Learning: A Probabilistic Perspective*. The MIT Press, 2012.

[MZV18] J. Martínez García, D. Zoeke, and M. Vossiek. Mimo-fmcw radar-based parking monitoring application with a modified convolutional neural network with spatial priors. *IEEE Access*, 6:41391–41398, 2018.

[Nar11] Ram M. Narayanan. Earthquake survivor detection using life signals from radar micro-doppler. In *Proceedings of the 1st International Conference on*

Wireless Technologies for Humanitarian Relief, ACWR '11, page 259–264, New York, NY, USA, 2011.

[PB20] R. Pérez and E. Biebl. 77GHz FMCW Radar Measurements in Urban Scenarios. [Dataset]. Available: `https://mediatum.ub.tum.de/1542227` [Accessed]: 07.05.2020, 2020.

[PBS08] Florian Pfeiffer, Erwin Biebl, and Karl-Heinz Siedersberger. *Determination of Complex Permittivity of LRR Radome Materials Using a Scalar Quasi-Optical Measurement System*, pages 205–210. Springer Berlin Heidelberg, Berlin, Heidelberg, 2008.

[PDKG20] A. Palffy, J. Dong, J. F. P. Kooij, and D. M. Gavrila. Cnn based road user detection using the 3d radar cube. *IEEE Robotics and Automation Letters*, 5(2):1263–1270, 2020.

[Pfe10] Florian Pfeiffer. *Analyse und Optimierung von Radomen für automobile Radarsensoren.* Cuvillier Verlag Göttingen, 2010.

[PG17] Josh Patterson and Adam Gibson. *Deep learning: A practitioner's approach.* O'Reilly Media, Inc., 2017.

[PHO+18] R. Prophet, M. Hoffmann, A. Ossowska, W. Malik, C. Sturm, and M. Vossiek. Image-based pedestrian classification for 79 ghz automotive radar. In *2018 15th European Radar Conference (EuRAD)*, pages 75–78, 2018.

[PHV+18] R. Prophet, M. Hoffmann, M. Vossiek, C. Sturm, A. Ossowska, W. Malik, and U. Lübbert. Pedestrian classification with a 79 ghz automotive radar sensor. In *2018 19th International Radar Symposium (IRS)*, pages 1–6, 2018.

[PJMK16] Jinhee Park, Rios Jesus Javier, Taesup Moon, and Youngwook Kim. Micro-doppler based classification of human aquatic activities via transfer learning of convolutional neural networks. *Sensors*, 16(12):1990, 2016.

[PLSV19] R. Prophet, G. Li, C. Sturm, and M. Vossiek. Semantic segmentation on automotive radar maps. In *2019 IEEE Intelligent Vehicles Symposium (IV)*, pages 756–763, 2019.

[Poz05] David M. Pozar. *Microwave Engineering.* John Wiley & Sons, Inc., 3rd edition edition, 2005.

[PRV+19] K. Patel, K. Rambach, T. Visentin, D. Rusev, M. Pfeiffer, and B. Yang. Deep learning-based object classification on automotive radar spectra. In *2019 IEEE Radar Conference (RadarConf)*, pages 1–6, 2019.

[PSRB18] R. Pérez, F. Schubert, R. Rasshofer, and E. Biebl. Single-Frame Vulnerable Road Users Classification with a 77 GHz FMCW Radar Sensor and a Convolutional Neural Network. In *International Radar Symposium (IRS)*, pages 1–10, 2018.

[PSRB19a] R. Pérez, F. Schubert, R. Rasshofer, and E. Biebl. A machine learning joint lidar and radar classification system in urban automotive scenarios. *Advances in Radio Science*, 17:129–136, 2019.

[PSRB19b] R. Pérez, F. Schubert, R. Rasshofer, and E. Biebl. Deep Learning Radar Object Detection and Classification for Urban Automotive Scenarios. In *2019 Kleinheubach Conference*, pages 1–4, Sep. 2019.

[PSRB21] R. Pérez, F. Schubert, R. Rasshofer, and E. Biebl. Range Detection on Time-Domain FMCW Radar Signals With a Deep Neural Network. *IEEE Sensors Letters*, 5(2):1–4, 2021.

[QYSG17] Charles Ruizhongtai Qi, Li Yi, Hao Su, and Leonidas J. Guibas. Pointnet++: Deep hierarchical feature learning on point sets in a metric space. *CoRR*, abs/1706.02413, 2017.

[RDGF15] Joseph Redmon, Santosh Kumar Divvala, Ross B. Girshick, and Ali Farhadi. You only look once: Unified, real-time object detection. *CoRR*, abs/1506.02640, 2015.

[RDS+15] Olga Russakovsky, Jia Deng, Hao Su, Jonathan Krause, Sanjeev Satheesh, Sean Ma, Zhiheng Huang, Andrej Karpathy, Aditya Khosla, Michael Bernstein, Alexander C. Berg, and Li Fei-Fei. ImageNet Large Scale Visual Recognition Challenge. *International Journal of Computer Vision (IJCV)*, 115(3):211–252, 2015.

[RF16] Joseph Redmon and Ali Farhadi. Yolo9000: Better, faster, stronger. *arXiv preprint arXiv:1612.08242*, 2016.

[RF18] Joseph Redmon and Ali Farhadi. Yolov3: An incremental improvement. *CoRR*, abs/1804.02767, 2018.

[RHGS15] Shaoqing Ren, Kaiming He, Ross B. Girshick, and Jian Sun. Faster R-CNN: towards real-time object detection with region proposal networks. *CoRR*, abs/1506.01497, 2015.

[RHR10] H. Rohling, S. Heuel, and H. Ritter. Pedestrian detection procedure integrated into an 24 ghz automotive radar. In *2010 IEEE Radar Conference*, pages 1229–1232, 2010.

[Ric14] Mark A. Richards. *Fundamentals of Radar Signal Processing, Second Edition.* McGraw-Hill, 2nd edition edition, 2014.

[Roh83] H. Rohling. Radar cfar thresholding in clutter and multiple target situations. *IEEE Transactions on Aerospace and Electronic Systems*, AES-19(4):608–621, 1983.

[Ros57] Frank Rosenblatt. The Perceptron — a Perceiving and Recognizing Automaton (Project PARA). Technical Report 85-460-1, Cornell Aeronautical Laboratory, Inc., January 1957.

[Ros61] Frank Rosenblatt. *Principles of neurodynamics. Perceptrons and the theory of brain mechanisms.* 1961.

[RR07] H. Ritter and H. Rohling. Pedestrian detection based on automotive radar. In *2007 IET International Conference on Radar Systems*, pages 1–4, 2007.

[Sha49] C. E. Shannon. Communication in the presence of noise. *Proceedings of the IRE*, 37(1):10–21, Jan 1949.

[SHDW18] O. Schumann, M. Hahn, J. Dickmann, and C. Wöhler. Semantic segmentation on radar point clouds. In *2018 21st International Conference on Information Fusion (FUSION)*, pages 2179–2186, 2018.

[SHK+14] Nitish Srivastava, Geoffrey Hinton, Alex Krizhevsky, Ilya Sutskever, and Ruslan Salakhutdinov. Dropout: a simple way to prevent neural networks from overfitting. *The journal of machine learning research*, 15(1):1929–1958, 2014.

[Sil84] Samuel Silver, editor. *Microwave Antenna Theory and Design.* IEE Electromagnetic Waves Series 19. Peter Peregrinus Ltd., 1984.

[SKFM14] E. Schubert, M. Kunert, A. Frischen, and W. Menzel. A multi-reflection-point target model for classification of pedestrians by automotive radar. In *2014 11th European Radar Conference*, pages 181–184, 2014.

[Sko01] Merrill I. Skolnik. *Introduction to Radar Systems.* Electrical engineering series. McGraw-Hill, 3rd edition edition, 2001.

[Sli20] A. P. Sligar. Machine learning-based radar perception for autonomous vehicles using full physics simulation. *IEEE Access*, 8:51470–51476, 2020.

[SLJ+15] Christian Szegedy, Wei Liu, Yangqing Jia, Pierre Sermanet, Scott Reed, Dragomir Anguelov, Dumitru Erhan, Vincent Vanhoucke, and Andrew Rabinovich. Going deeper with convolutions. In *Computer Vision and Pattern Recognition (CVPR)*, 2015.

[SMB10] Dominik Scherer, Andreas Müller, and Sven Behnke. Evaluation of pooling operations in convolutional architectures for object recognition. In *International conference on artificial neural networks*, pages 92–101. Springer, 2010.

[SMKM15a] E. Schubert, F. Meinl, M. Kunert, and W. Menzel. Clustering of high resolution automotive radar detections and subsequent feature extraction for classification of road users. In *2015 16th International Radar Symposium (IRS)*, pages 174–179, 2015.

[SMKM15b] E. Schubert, F. Meinl, M. Kunert, and W. Menzel. High resolution automotive radar measurements of vulnerable road users – pedestrians & cyclists. In *2015 IEEE MTT-S International Conference on Microwaves for Intelligent Mobility (ICMIM)*, pages 1–4, April 2015.

[SSM+17] M. Stolz, E. Schubert, F. Meinl, M. Kunert, and W. Menzel. Multi-target reflection point model of cyclists for automotive radar. In *2017 European Radar Conference (EURAD)*, pages 94–97, 2017.

[SUF18] A. Santra, R. V. Ulaganathan, and T. Finke. Short-range millimetric-wave radar system for occupancy sensing application. *IEEE Sensors Letters*, 2(3):1–4, Sep. 2018.

[SWB06] G. E. Smith, K. Woodbridge, and C. J. Baker. Micro-doppler signature classification. In *2006 CIE International Conference on Radar*, pages 1–4, Oct 2006.

[SZ14] Karen Simonyan and Andrew Zisserman. Very deep convolutional networks for large-scale image recognition. *CoRR*, abs/1409.1556, 2014.

[TBFA05] S. Thrun, W. Burgard, D. Fox, and R.C. Arkin. *Probabilistic Robotics*. Intelligent robotics and autonomous agents. MIT Press, Cambridge, Massachusetts, USA, 2005.

[TSK+18] Chuanqi Tan, Fuchun Sun, Tao Kong, Wenchang Zhang, Chao Yang, and Chunfang Liu. A survey on deep transfer learning. *CoRR*, abs/1808.01974, 2018.

[vG03] P. van Dorp and F. C. A. Groen. Human walking estimation with radar. *IEE Proceedings - Radar, Sonar and Navigation*, 150(5):356–365, Oct 2003.

[VGKN09] L. Vignaud, A. Ghaleb, J. L. Kernec, and J. Nicolas. Radar high resolution range micro-doppler analysis of human motions. In *2009 International Radar Conference "Surveillance for a Safer World" (RADAR 2009)*, pages 1–6, Oct 2009.

[VL14] Andrea Vedaldi and Karel Lenc. Matconvnet - convolutional neural networks for MATLAB. *CoRR*, abs/1412.4564, 2014.

[WTL19] L. Wang, J. Tang, and Q. Liao. A study on radar target detection based on deep neural networks. *IEEE Sensors Letters*, 3(3):1–4, 2019.

[ZWCD19] Long Zhou, Suyuan Wei, Zhongma Cui, and Wei Ding. YOLO-RD: A lightweight object detection network for range doppler radar images. *IOP Conference Series: Materials Science and Engineering*, 563:042027, aug 2019.

[ZZXW19] Z. Zhao, P. Zheng, S. Xu, and X. Wu. Object detection with deep learning: A review. *IEEE Transactions on Neural Networks and Learning Systems*, 30(11):3212–3232, 2019.

Own Publications

[EPR19] N. Engelhardt, R. Pérez, and Q. Rao. Occupancy Grids Generation Using Deep Radar Network for Autonomous Driving. In *2019 IEEE Intelligent Transportation Systems Conference (ITSC)*, pages 2866–2871, Oct 2019.

[PB20] R. Pérez and E. Biebl. 77GHz FMCW Radar Measurements in Urban Scenarios. [Dataset]. Available: `https://mediatum.ub.tum.de/1542227` [Accessed]: 07.05.2020, 2020.

[PSRB18] R. Pérez, F. Schubert, R. Rasshofer, and E. Biebl. Single-Frame Vulnerable Road Users Classification with a 77 GHz FMCW Radar Sensor and a Convolutional Neural Network. In *International Radar Symposium (IRS)*, pages 1–10, 2018.

[PSRB19a] R. Pérez, F. Schubert, R. Rasshofer, and E. Biebl. A machine learning joint lidar and radar classification system in urban automotive scenarios. *Advances in Radio Science*, 17:129–136, 2019.

[PSRB19b] R. Pérez, F. Schubert, R. Rasshofer, and E. Biebl. Deep Learning Radar Object Detection and Classification for Urban Automotive Scenarios. In *2019 Kleinheubach Conference*, pages 1–4, Sep. 2019.

[PSRB21] R. Pérez, F. Schubert, R. Rasshofer, and E. Biebl. Range Detection on Time-Domain FMCW Radar Signals With a Deep Neural Network. *IEEE Sensors Letters*, 5(2):1–4, 2021.

[WPB20] J. Weiß, R. Pérez, and E. Biebl. Improved People Counting Algorithm for Indoor Environments using 60 GHz FMCW Radar. In *2020 IEEE Radar Conference (RadarConf20)*, pages 1–6, 2020.

www.ingramcontent.com/pod-product-compliance
Ingram Content Group UK Ltd.
Pitfield, Milton Keynes, MK11 3LW, UK
UKHW022000190726
13853UKWH00004B/1637

9 783736 974623